Cluster of Billionaires

"A computer cluster consists of a set of loosely or tightly connected computers that work together so that, in many respects, they can be viewed as a single system."

From Wikipedia, the free encyclopedia

I0413609

By Yuri Barzov

2017

Table of contents

4

Acknowledgments

I thank Anton Derlyatka, Vadim Cherdak, Pavel Cherkashin, Sergey Chistyakov, Mark Fedin, Mikhail Ivanov, Sergey Litovchenko, Pavel Loznevoy, Andrey Lubalin, Lyubov Nazarova, Katerina Oparysheva and Igor Salita for supporting this book's crowdfunding campaign thus encouraging me to finish it.

I thank Ivan Sukhy for proofreading this book and giving me the most valuable feedback and advice.

Prologue

Do you want to be a billionaire? Who on Earth doesn't want to have billions of dollars? The right answer is counter intuitive at least. The future billionaires.

Yvon Chouinard, the founder of Patagonia, a giant outdoor gear company, was born in 1938 in Lisbon, Maine. His family moved to Burbank, California, when he was about eight. When he was 14 Chouinard joined a falconry club. At 16, he spent the summer in Wyoming climbing rocks and he really got passionate about it. "For the better part of his 20s, Yvon Chouinard spent more than half of each year gallivanting across North America and the Alps, sometimes living on 50 cents a day, as he climbed peaks with his buddies. The man who would later go on to found outdoor gear titan Patagonia would catch ground squirrels to supplement his diet and sometimes hide out from rangers when he overstayed camping limits at parks." Daniela Sirtori-Cortina wrote of him in Forbes when he in 2017 was finally declared a billionaire against his own will.

Patagonia strongly opposed Chouinard being included on the billionaires list because its founder didn't even want to be called a businessman not speaking about a billionaire. "I've been a businessman for almost sixty years. It's as difficult for me to say those words as it is for someone to admit being an alcoholic or a lawyer. I've never respected the profession." Chouinard wrote in the introduction to a revised 2016 edition of his 2005 memoir-manifesto book Let My People Go Surfing.

Chouinard is not the only billionaire who built his business around his passion instead of being passionate about business. "I always think that this is kind of a perverse thing about Silicon

Valley in a way that people decide often that they want to start a company before they even decide what they want to do." Mark Zuckerberg admitted to Sam Altman of YCombinator in their How to Build the Future interview series.

Some of them like co-founder of Apple Steve Jobs speak about passion. Others like co-founder of PayPal Peter Thiel prefer to call it calling emphasising that they are moved by something that can make life better but not just something that they are passionate about. Yet another name for the same phenomena is purpose. They do not chose their passion, passion choses them, as the founder of Amazon Jeff Bezos elegantly put it.

In March 2017, Snap, the holding company of Snapchat instant photo messaging platform made an IPO. The company, which has never earned a profit, was valued by the market at 24 billion dollars. Millennials bought shares on the stock exchange simply because they like Snapchat. Snapchat's co-founder Evan Spiegel and his partner became multi-billionaires. In an interview two years earlier Evan, answering the question, which decision was the most difficult for him, said: "The hardest part was to refuse Facebook's offer to sell the company for $ 3 billion in 2013." Curiously, Facebook founder and CEO Mark Zuckerberg, responding to the same question in 2016 interview with Sam Altman, said that the hardest thing for him was to refuse to sell the company for a billion dollars to Yahoo in 2007. Both stated that money was not the main motive for them. They just wanted to make a truly cool product for people.

Future billionaires do not chase billions. At least the vast majority of self made billionaires didn't. How can it be possible? All rich people are greedy. They became rich because they love money more than anything else. Everyone knows it. These statements sound logical. While we are fair towards our peers we tend to judge billionaires by their wealth as if they are defined by money. Such attitude is strongly biased. What if we try to take the bias away?

Our world is full of people who are explaining to others things which they don't understand themselves. I am writing this book not because I want to explain to you something but because I want to better understand this subject myself. It is easier for me to do it by writing. I shall draw conclusions only when I come to the end of this book. I share it with you so that we can together walk our way to understanding. It is more interesting to do it together. It is highly likely that each of us will reach his or her own understanding. I guess, we can start now.

The Queens' Race

"My dear, here we must run as fast as we can, just to stay in place. And if you wish to go anywhere you must run twice as fast as that."

From Alice in Wonderland by Lewis Carroll.

The ritualised 'winner-winner' fighting of one species of ants transforms a group of its participants into gamergates — worker queens. Gamergates look just like ordinary workers but undergo extreme internal changes, according to research from North Carolina State University, Arizona State University and the U.S. Department of Agriculture. Increased dopamine levels in brains of fighting ants trigger significant changes in their physiology without any related changes to their DNA. The transformation is caused by existing genes turning on and off.

Billionaire is a condition similar to gamergate. It can be achieved by taking part in a kind of race. Not every member of the cluster of billionaires controls billions but all self made billionaires are members of this cluster. Each of them actually joined the race in the cluster long before making billions.

"For me the mandate is just to grow as fast as humanly possible." Evan Spiegel, Co-founder and CEO of Snapchat said answering to the question about his leadership priorities on the Code Conference in 2015. He was only 24 years old then.

"I started doing cross country running when I was in an elementary school. And in a cross country running you gonna have to be on this border of aerobic and anaerobic. Anaerobic needs you need more oxygen. Aerobic means you have enough. And you have to stay on this line. And you have to have endurance." Travis Kalanick, co-founder and CEO of Uber was explaining to Arianna Huffington, founder of Huffington Post. "But you also is trying to go as fast as you can. You are trying to beat your own personal record." He used his childhood memories to illustrate his current approach to business; or even more broadly to life.

Anyone can enter the cluster of billionaires just by starting a special sort of a long term race. Like ritualised fights of gamergates the race may be tough but it doesn't produce any losers. You can start running with a speed that suits you best. You are winning as long as you keep running. If you stop, you just drop off into the cluster of consumers that might finally be a much more comfortable and pleasant place for you.

Runners can be stopped by the spectators. If an ant undergoing the transformation into the gamergate is moved from the colony where the battle took place into another ant colony, local ants will recognize the changes and apply 'policing' actions in respect of the transforming ant. They will be holding the transforming ant down so that it can't move. Within 24 hours dopamine levels of transforming ants get back to normal and they are just ordinary workers again.

Members of the cluster stick together to increase each other's potential in this neverending race that produces only winners. By running close to each other they manage to attract more resources. Thus more consolidated this cluster becomes, the more billionaires it produces.

In the past the consolidation of this cluster was slowed down by long distances, national borders, religious, social, political, informational barriers. When the members of the cluster run alone among the resting consumers they might be stopped and held in place by the consumers until they turn into consumers themselves. Their behavior looks abnormal from the consumer's point of view. Consumers just mean good when they are stopping the running individuals but it may be painful to be abruptly stopped and thrown to the ground. Running together increases safety and speed. Therefore interconnection is the key for the members of the cluster of billionaires to keep running.

Billions help the members of the cluster of billionaires to increase their speed to the point where they can no longer be stopped. Now when all barriers are coming down and the world becomes smaller and better connected, maybe, soon the time will come when each member of the cluster of billionaires will control billions.

An Invisible Wall

Belonging to the cluster is not formalized in any way but an invisible wall separates the cluster from the rest of the world. Anyone can join or leave. Talking through the wall about weather is also possible. The exchange of meaningful information between those who are inside and those who are outside is simply impossible. People from the cluster absolutely unintentionally assign different meanings to commonly used words. Psychology and neuroscience professor of Princeton University Uri Hasson demonstrates in his research how it is possible.

In his lab in Princeton, Hasson and his team take people to the fMRI scanner and scan their brains while they are either telling or listening to real-life stories. Their results indicate that during successful communication the speaker's and listener's brains exhibit joint, temporally coupled, response patterns. Such neural coupling substantially diminishes in the absence of communication, for instance, when listening to an unintelligible foreign language. In addition, more extensive neural couplings between speaker and listener result in more successful communication.

According to Hasson, our ability to communicate also relies on our ability to have a common ground. "This alignment depends not only on our ability to understand the basic concept; it also depends on our ability to develop common ground and understanding and shared belief systems. Because we know that in many cases, people understand the exact same story in very different ways." Hasson says.

Just changing the context is enough to make people to understand exactly the same narrative in entirely different way.

Within its own common ground and shared belief system the cluster of billionaires uses its own language that can't be understood by anybody outside the cluster.

"Everyone is entitled to their own perception of me." Says Evan Spiegel, co-founder and CEO of Snapchat with a reputation of an arrogant LA dude created by media. "I just try really hard to be me." Spiegel says that it is important for the popularity of Snapchat that he shows his unfiltered real himself. The media yet demands him to show a filtered hypocritical image of himself to be a role model for the right, meaning hypocritical, behaviour to 'ordinary people.' Mark Zuckerberg of Facebook, Travis Kalanick of Uber and many more self made billionaires of today are faced with the same challenge. They respond by trying to genuinely change their interface for the better. There is no evidence, however, that the improved versions of themselves will be able to achieve what they have achieved. I will focus in this book in the first place on the behaviours of the members of the cluster which help them to achieve significant and sustainable changes in their brains. We will talk about them adapting to the role of real billionaires later, if we have time.

Authenticity is the context of the cluster of billionaires. You can't fake it until you make it. We all come into this world authentic.

A Planet of Ants

Do all ants combined outweigh all humans combined? Some scientists claim they do. Others believe that humans outweighed ants roughly at the time when America became independent (1776). All scientists basically agree, however, that ants rule the world.   Indeed, ants have colonised almost every landmass on Earth, and can survive at the extremes of the natural world. In the Sahara desert, shiny silver ants search the scorching desert sands to scavenge corpses of heat-stricken animals, before racing back to their nests to avoid overheating themselves. At the opposite extreme near the Arctic Circle, thatch ants build and live in their own centrally-heated rotting compost heaps. When floodwaters from the Amazon River submerge their rainforest homes, fire ants will grasp each other to form a living raft that floats the colony to safety.

Ants outnumber us 1.5 million to one. This abundance of ants around the world makes them a dominant force in nature. Like us, ant colonies have the capacity to build their own world around them. Ants can do it because they have a short range but exceptionally efficient and fast communication system. Spitting pheromones, hormones and proteins enables them to create superorganisms with significant cognitive abilities.

Termites - close relatives of ants - are remarkable construction workers, capable of building mounds standing more than 30 feet (10 metres) high and 40 feet (15 metres) wide at their base. Termites use the same structures for millennia. In 2015 in the Miombo woodland area of central Africa, scientists have found a termite mound that is more than 2200 years old. It was abandoned but the study reveals termites regularly used it 800 to

500 years ago. Mounds have a lifespan that is more than compatible with the length of life of human cities.

When termites build their mounds they don't have a plan. It turns out there is no head engineer or master architect directing the hundreds of thousands of termites running around, says Judith Korb, a professor at the University of Regensburg, Germany. A termite will grab one soil particle, mix it with water and pheromone infused saliva and cement it in place. The next termite will come along and put its soil blob down next to the previous one, and this continues until eventually a wall is built. However, soon there are too many termites walking around with soil blobs, and this results in a termite traffic jam. At that point, termites give up and just drop their blobs where they are. Then another termite blob-drops next to them, beginning another structure. Eventually walls and tunnels connect, and at some point, a mound almost magically appears. Order emerges out of chaos.

Harvard professor of robotics Radhika Nagpal makes an analogy between the behavior of termites and the brain. Individual termites react rather than think, but at a group level they exhibit a kind of cognition and awareness of their surroundings. Similarly, in the brain, individual neurons don't think, but thinking arises in the connections between them.

Researchers of the behavior of ants also draw parallels with the nervous response systems of single organisms. "Just as we may respond to cell damage via pain, ant colonies respond to the loss of individuals via group awareness and reaction." Explains Thomas O'Shea-Wheller from the University of Bristol.

Earth hadn't always been a planet of ants. Scientists estimate that ancestors of modern-day ants first evolved about 160 million years ago. The fossil records suggest however that ants weren't dominating the planet until 60 million years later, when with the emergence of flowers, also known as angiosperms, these resilient insects, now found in almost all terrestrial ecosystems finally took the world over. "An event happened 100 million years ago and ants started diversifying like crazy," Corrie Moreau of Harvard University told LiveScience. "This is also the time when we start seeing the first angiosperm forests."

Order out of Chaos

An event is happening on our planet right now that might make human species dominant on more than just one planet. New order is emerging out of chaos as usually. Millions of migrants are on the move. Old power of elites is deteriorating. New players -- people from lower social stratas or God-forsaken wild borderlands -- are making it into the elites with a speed of launching space rockets. Many emperors become naked with an unparalleled speed. Privileged revolt against unprivileged turning the balance of power upside down. A nature of the power itself is changing.

Many people try to predict the outcome of these multifaceted chaotic processes. Some are suggesting the new division of people into castes according to their degree of ambitions and creativity will evolve. Others predict the coming of meritocracy. Third proclaim the rise of holacracy. Fourth preach Autonomous Decentralized Organizations built on blockchain. Each claims they present the only right and accurate positive order prediction for the future. Dystopias in the spirit of Orwell's 1984 are just innumerable.

Preachers are not welcome in the cluster of billionaires. Instead of calling humanity to a brighter future, the members of the cluster are busy with simply building it. Sometimes, however, we can see some blinks from them like the article Generation of Indigo written by the Russian billionaire Mikhail Fridman. This way billionaires -- just like termites drop their blobs of soil glued with pheromone rich saliva -- give a signal to their brothers and sisters by the cluster: "You are not idiots. It's exactly how you see it. Screw it, just do it!"

"We are entering a disruptive era driven by extraordinary levels of human creativity. A new generation of curious, strong-willed and talented individuals is unhindered by convention or the past... This is an era where abnormally talented individuals and entities are now able to realize new levels of human potential and economic achievement." Fridman writes. Further we will see that the individuals coined by Fridman as 'abnormally talented' are not abnormally talented after all. They are just normally talented. They just come from the cluster of billionaires. To prove this claim I will share with you the results of over twenty years of research and observation of the most noticeable members of the cluster of billionaires -- the actual billionaires themselves -- in dynamics of their development.

Right now when I am writing these lines the humankind is splitting into two unequal clusters: the cluster of billionaires and the cluster of consumers. Moreover, this separation does not take place on the basis of wealth, power or social status; not even on the basis of ownership of the means of production. The old realities are generally irrelevant to this split.

The basis of the new division is a threshold increase in some people of the efficiency of use of their main resources -- their brain and their time. People who have passed the threshold, are consolidating in the cluster of billionaires. Those who remain beyond the threshold, form the cluster of consumers. There is nothing humiliating to consumers or offensive for billionaires in this division. The new structure will be similar to the colony of ants.

When we watch termites moving back and forth busily it is hard to imagine that 80 percent of them, as research suggests, do absolutely nothing. "As a group, they always look busy. But as individuals, only a few of them actually spend their time digging."

Says Brian Forschler, a researcher with the UGA College of Agricultural and Environmental Sciences. It doesn't prevent the remaining 20 percent of hard working termites from building their up to 30 feet tall mounds. Hard workers and loafers alike are then living in the nest under that mound.

A similar order is governing in colonies of ants which thank's to the Aesop's Fable "The Grasshopper and the Ants" are believed to be the most industrious creatures on Earth. In reality most ants in a colony are doing nothing. Researchers discovered that out of all ants which were classified as workers, 71.9% were inactive at least half the time, and 25.1% were never seen working, just 2.6%, were always active during observation. As ant group grows in size, so does the number of inactive members, scientists say. In groups of 30 ants, 60 percent of ants were idle, while in groups of 300 ants already 80 percent of the critters were doing nothing.

Thus the size of the cluster of billionaires should be somewhere in the range of 3-20% of the total population of humanity to effortlessly provide a comfortable existence to everyone and to direct all the rest of its exponentially growing resources for the achievement of its goals.

Evolving information society strangely wrenches and reinforces phenomena that has been present in our lives always. Billionaires have always existed as exceptions. The cluster of billionaires also existed. The difference of the current moment is only in the fact that it began to consolidate. Worldwide penetration of Internet and mobile communications gave to this consolidation a truly planetary scale. Its core is gaining critical mass, drawing to the cluster more and more neophytes. That results in a traffic jam. Like termites members of the cluster give up trying to get to the core and start their projects (drop their blobs) where they are.

Then another member of the cluster 'blob-drops' next to them, beginning another node of the emerging network.

Struck Heads

Our world is changing rapidly. While this may sound like a platitude only a few can feel the real speed and scale of changes. Who are the lucky ones who are able to not only keep up with the changes, but also to get ahead, to anticipate them? Digital nomads? New technological elite? Names are many, but none conveys the exact meaning. Malcolm Gladwell in his book calls them "Outliers". And they are really outliers. Now, before our very eyes outliers begin to form the trend. North America mints a new billionaire every six days. According to Credit Suisse's 2016 global wealth report it will continue minting them with the same speed for the next five years. While China is still far behind North America the population of Chinese billionaires is growing fast. So far we count them in hundreds. It is always this way in the beginning of an exponential growth when the base for doubling is still very small. Absolute numbers are not impressive but they are already doubling. Year 2016 was another record year for Forbes as the number of billionaires in its 2017 list grew 13% to 2,043 from 1,810 in 2016. The first time ever the number of billionaires in Forbes list exceeded 2,000. The gain in the number of billionaires -- up 233 since the 2016 list -- was the biggest in the entire 31 years' period for which Forbes has been tracking billionaires globally. Gainers since last year's list outnumbered losers by more than three to one.

The chances of anyone becoming a billionaire are still quite low but they are growing.

So how anyone can become a billionaire? First you need to get to the cluster of billionaires. Then you have to find some other members of the cluster like you and couple your brains with theirs. And then, four years after joining the cluster (3-5 with adjustment for luck): "bar-boom!" -- billions will magically appear as if on a silver platter in front of you. But all this will happen later. The cluster comes first.

Self made billionaires remind me peculiar freshly minted coins. They all are same size and made from the same material. All, however, have different portraits shown on their head side and different constantly changing values struck on the other.

What are they, the minted members of the cluster of billionaires in the first place? Perhaps, they all have charisma -- a trait often associated with being extroverted? From the beginning entrepreneurs tend to do better when they're charismatic and extroverted. Being social and outgoing helps leaders make more connections, inspire their employees, earn trust faster and grow their audience. Extroverts easily go out to networking events and meet new people there. The entrepreneurial lifestyle is chaotic and noisy one -- something only extroverts enjoy.

"You know, it was not like show on Shark Tank. Zuckerberg was nineteen years old and pretty introverted. Sean did most of the talking. So if you base... People always exaggerate how important these pitch meetings are. Reid Hoffman and I had spent almost a year looking at all these social networking sites before that. So we were ready to write a check before we met. It didn't really matter what people were going to say." An early investor in Facebook and a co-founder of PayPal and of the secretive 15 billion dollar startup Palantir Peter Thiel recalls this way his first meeting with the co-founders of Facebook Mark Zuckerberg and Sean Parker (Sean became famous by founding Napster - the music sharing startup that totally disrupted the musical industry before it was shut down by court). Reid Hoffman is a co-founder of LinkedIn -- a business social networking startup that went public and was acquired by Microsoft in 2016 for some 28 billion dollars. Four members of the cluster of billionaires were present in that meeting but none of them is a naturally born charismatic extrovert if we judge by their video available in big quantity on the internet.

Co-founder of Google Larry Page is highly reserved, and "geeky." The founder of Microsoft and the wealthiest person on Earth according to Forbes Bill Gates started out as a solitary introvert. The founder of Berkshire Hathaway from the top of billionaires' list Warren Buffett is famous for his intellectual level-headedness and introversion. The founder of Tesla, Space-X and Solarcity, one of the first shareholders of PayPal Elon Musk was once a reserved introverted engineer. He was the member of the cluster of billionaires already then. None of these people has really changed over years so much to become extroverts from introverts. What is the secret? The answer is twofold. First, they have other members of the cluster who are naturally born good talkers in their nodes of the cluster. Second, with time they managed to develop their own public presentation skills to a very impressive level.

The Oracle of Omaha Learns to Speak

"The Oracle of Omaha, Warren Buffett ranked number two on the Forbes 400 for 15 years straight. That streak ended in September 2016 when he was overtaken (by Jeff Bezos) despite adding $3.5 billion to his fortune in the previous year... Known for his relative frugality, Buffett still lives in the Omaha home he purchased for $31,500 in 1958. He says his best investment was buying Benjamin Graham's legendary book, "The Intelligent Investor," in 1949." Forbes writes about #3 Forbes 400 (2016).

"I was so terrified that I just couldn't speak in public... I would throw up... In fact, I arranged my life so that I never had to get up in front of anybody." Warren Buffett told his biographer Alice Schroeder in "The Snowball: Warren Buffett and the Business of Life." After moving back to Omaha after grad school, he saw an ad in the paper for a Dale Carnegie speaking course. Buffett trusted Carnegie, whose book "How To Win Friends and Influence People," he believed, changed his life. He signed up for the course. The class met at a hotel in Omaha. There were about 30 students who were all just terrified. They got a book of speeches and had to deliver one of those speeches every week. Buffett got lots of experience speaking to a group of people in a low-stakes situation. The students supported one another, and slowly, slowly, slowly, Buffett got comfortable in front of a crowd. "Some of it is just practice — just doing it and practicing. And it worked. That's the most important degree I have." Buffett said.

Not too many billionaires are as candid with their interviewers as Peter Thiel or Warren Buffett. It is hard for them to explain how they became billionaires because they don't know the exact answer themselves. They still are constantly asked about secrets of their success. Very balanced and beautiful corporate legends often evolve in response. The heroes of these legends frequently end up believing themselves in that cleverly tailored and neatly cut stuff. In reality they are not thousand times more honest or hardworking than other people. They are not blessed with a greater intellect or a wider range of emotions than others. They have the usual human weaknesses and vices. However, they as members of the same cluster are still united by only one, but very important behavioral trait that allows them to compress time, enabling them to achieve orders of magnitude more than the others.

From Zero to One billion in Four Years

So was named brand new consulting product of McKinsey that Alexey Reznikovich, then partner of this glorious company, and now Managing Partner of Letter One Technology belonging to Mikhail Fridman, and me tried to promote among Russian customers at the turn of the millennium. McKinsey Institute had seriously studied the experience of several dozens of companies, which had reached a billion dollar capitalization in the last decades of the 20th century. We proposed to help building a billion dollar company by utilizing the findings of this study. McKinsey picked the timeframe out of the blue - not a very short (the client would not believe), and not too long (the client would not want to wait so long). I think then the four years timespan was the ideal case scenario, and an average term was closer to ten years. Now it is shorter and is continuing to decline because the connection between all people on the planet, including the members of the cluster of billionaires, is becoming closer and the "friend or foe" recognition is happening almost instantaneously.

"We didn't assemble a mafia by sorting through résumés and simply hiring the most talented people" Peter Thiel writes in his book From Zero to One about the famous PayPal mafia. Then he continues to try to explain an entirely new phenomena with conventional words.

The project Reznikovich and I worked on was about companies, not people, but the main message, that all depends on the team, was absolutely correct. Only we then all together in agreement absolutely missed the selection criteria of the team required to achieve the billion because we relied on all kinds of models of management and leadership competencies and, of course, were too clever by half. As it turned out, you do not have to be a leader or a manager to get to the cluster of billionaires. It is not necessary to know anything about doing business at all for joining the cluster. But you must train your brain to work in the second order that ensures its radical plasticity. But then we did not even know such words.

The French Patient

A decade ago Axel Cleeremans, a cognitive psychologist from the Université Libre de Bruxelles in Belgium came across a very interesting case. A Frenchman who was then 44 years old only went to the doctor complaining of mild weakness in his left leg. Brain scans revealed that his skull was mostly filled with fluid, leaving just a thin outer layer of actual brain tissue, with the internal part of his brain almost totally eroded away. Doctors were surprised to see that despite his minimal remaining brain tissue, the man wasn't mentally disabled - he had a low IQ of 75, but was working as a civil servant. He was also married with two children, and was relatively healthy.

Not only did this case cause scientists to question what it takes to survive, it also challenged our understanding of consciousness. In the past, researchers have suggested that consciousness might be linked to various specific brain regions - such as the claustrum, a thin sheet of neurons running between major brain regions, or the visual cortex. But if those hypotheses were correct, then the French man shouldn't be conscious, with the majority of these areas being diminished in his brain to nonexistence.

In order to explain how the French patient stayed conscious Cleeremans came up with a hypothesis that the brain learns to be conscious. He claims, that as such, few specific neural features are necessary for consciousness, since areas of the brain are able to adapt and develop consciousness. "Consciousness is the brain's non-conceptual theory about itself, gained through experience—that is learning, interacting with itself, the world, and with other people," he says.

In the summer of 2016, a decade after the publication of the first results, Axel presented at the international neuroscientists Congress in Buenos Aires, his concept of "radical plasticity" - the state which is achieved in the brains of adults by activating the meta-cognition neural network, which controls the process of learning in first order networks which are processing primary input information - those which perceive signals from senses. Namely this meta-cognition network allows our brain to distinguish between what we know, what we do not know, and to handle the known and the unknown data in different ways. Axel also named this meta cognition network second order network to underline the hierarchical nature of consciousness.

The existence of metacognition network has been recently confirmed experimentally. A group of researchers from the Université Libre de Bruxelles and the University of Amsterdam investigated the relationship between metacognitive performance and first-order task performance by recording EEG signals while participants were asked to perform first order tasks and metacognitive assessments of their performance. The experiment proved that different networks are activated when the brain processes first order information and makes metacognitive judgements. Furthermore, results demonstrated that the information that contributes to first-order decisions differs from the information that supports metacognitive (second order) judgments.

By observing the cognition practices of members of the cluster of billionaires we will soon find out that they had developed in particular the ability to accelerate the performance of their second order network to an unprecedented level. At the same time, the second order network lowers wiring costs due to its special architecture, reminiscent of computer models of small-worlds and scale-free networks.

Is Your Brain Really Necessary?

A paper written by Roger Lewin for Science Magazine in December 1980 was titled 'Is Your Brain Really Necessary?' John Lorber, a British neurologist, described in it worked with another patient with virtually no brain. Like the French patient of Axel Cleeremans the patient of John Lorber had hydrocephalus. His cranium was filled mainly with cerebrospinal fluid. Only 5% of his brain tissue was left. Unlike the French patient who had low IQ of 75 the British patient had IQ of 126. The Englishman with virtually no brain earned a first class honours degree in mathematics. As the Frenchman he was socially completely normal.

Three decades after Lewin's paper, in 2012, Brazilian neurosurgeon Matheus Fernandes de Oliveira et al in their paper advocated research into computational models such as the small-world and scale-free network as the possible reasons for cognitive and social normality of some hydrocephalic no brainers.

In small-world networks neuronal cells are engaged in clustered connectivity with fewer long-range connections. Thus, there is a shorter path length between any pair of neurons or brain regions, resulting in higher dynamical complexity, lower wiring costs, and resilience to tissue insults. A scale-free network is characterized by the existence of a small number of nodes having more connections than the other nodes. The nodes that have such a high connectivity degree are referred to as hub-nodes and play an important role in the overall network organization.

The point of the paper was that under the right conditions, a brain damage may paradoxically result in a brain enhancement.

Small-world and scale-free network architectures by overlapping and mutually enhancing each other may turbocharge just a fraction of a brain into performing like the whole thing.

Why then scientists didn't pursue this idea further since de Oliveira et al published it in 2012? It's because it was commonly assumed for the past 15 plus years that a normal brain is already a small-world network. Recent studies suggest however that, at cellular resolution, the brain may be a large-world network, rather than a classical small-world network. Even more importantly, the organization of the brain may produce different network topologies under different circumstances.

Now just imagine a normal sized brain working at the performance level of a turbocharged no brainer. This is exactly what happens with the brains of members of the cluster of billionaires.

Who Is Selected for Astronauts?

"Born in the Ukraine, raised in Moscow and schooled in America, Len Blavatnik emigrated to the U.S. in 1978, earning degrees from Columbia U. and Harvard Business School. He became a citizen in 1984 and now stands atop a global empire, which includes assets in commodities production (LyondellBasell), technology (Rocket Internet) and media (Warner Music). Blavatnik made a fortune selling his stake in Russian oil company TNK-BP for $7 billion in 2013." Forbes about #22 in Forbes 400 2016.

I can't recall the exact date when I started to explore the cluster of billionaires. Maybe, it all started in late 1990-ties when I began to work with Roustam Tariko, the founder of the Russian Standard bank and the creator of a premium vodka brand under the same name. Or it started when the legendary inventor of cinemobile Fouad Said paid a visit to our office on Trekhgorny pereulok in Moscow? Or, maybe, when my then partner Sergey Vorobiev introduced me to Len Blavatnik, the current owner of Warner Music Group? One thing that I am sure about is that I was always interested to learn how did they make their billions. I wanted to know which qualities a person should possess to become a self made billionaire like them. I worked with all of them as an executive search consultant. I interviewed some of them with passion, extorting their secrets. With some we even went to vacations together. Sometimes it seemed to me that I was close to the answer, but it has always escaped. Now, in hindsight, I think that there has always been a barrier of incomprehension. It was absolutely invisible and this invisibility only aggravated mistrust and conflict.

Some of my friends called their bosses-billionaires people from the matrix, and argued that they needed an interpreter to communicate with normal people. In another business conglomerate local billionaires-oligarchs got the name "astronauts", which emphasized their detachment from earthly realities. Subordinates treated the "whim" of their billionaires differently. Some played along. Others argued or even fought for their right; for the interests of their companies, as they believed. In one organization an irreconcilable conflict between the founder and the management emerged, looking as if it was due to differences in their opinions on business strategy. This organization doesn't exist anymore. Interested to know the cause? Only one or maximum two people in leadership teams of almost all major companies and groups belonged to the cluster of billionaires. Other people on the team simply couldn't understand them.

The CEO and the VP for Marketing of the beverages distribution business Roust Inc. of Roustam Tariko were strongly frustrated. They complained to me each single day that Roustam again was cheating them with bonuses, which were linked to the increase of the net profit margin of the company. Indeed, Roustam rejected to count as the increase in the net profit margin some savings which they made by cutting advertising and recruitment budgets. His logic was very clear: he considered advertising as an investment into the brand of the company and recruitment as an investment into the future of the company. By not spending agreed amounts of money on these activities top managers were eating into the future of the company and its brand. In his view such savings of costs were a pure mistake of the company's management that could not be possibly rewarded by bonuses. So he suggested to adjust the formula of the calculation of bonuses. It was just a clarification for him not a change in the rules.

The top managers were afraid to discuss this matter with Roustam because deep inside they realized that he was right. But they were actively gossiping that Roustam was cheating because Roustam was right only in principle but according to the letter of their contracts they still believed they were entitled to be paid a bonus for their mistake. In this particular case, the letter proved to be on the side of Roustam after all because their bonuses were subject to approval by the board of directors, and the board voted in Roustam's favor. However, this case shows, in my view, quite clearly the difference between the cluster thinking and the non-cluster thinking. The facts were exactly the same but the context differed dramatically. Often people attribute this difference to the roles of business owner and employed manager. I have met during my already long life enough non owners with the cluster thinking to be sure that this division of thinking is not defined by ownership. The number of business owners who were incapable of the cluster thinking whom I met too, just reinforces this conclusion.

A Lifelong Trip

"Russia's most influential tech investor, Yuri Milner, was an early backer of Facebook and Twitter through his venture fund, DST Global. He sold those stakes but later invested in Spotify and Airbnb. He also bet big on Chinese tech companies, including online retailers Alibaba and JD. Com, and led multiple funding rounds in mobile phone maker Xiaomi. A former physicist, Milner joined Google's Sergey Brin and Facebook's Mark Zuckerberg in 2012 to found the Breakthrough Prize, which rewards top scientists with lucrative prizes and a glitzy awards ceremony. In July 2015, he launched "Breakthrough Listen," a $100 million project to search for alien life. "The biggest questions of our existence are at stake," he wrote in an open letter cosigned by eminent physicist Stephen Hawking, Family Guy creator Seth MacFarlane and others." Forbes writes about #544 at its Billionaires list of 2017.

An increasing number of twenty-somethings in Silicon Valley are reportedly 'micro-dosing' on psychedelic drugs - and they say it's making them better workers.

According to Rolling Stone a microdose is about a tenth of the normal dose – around 10 micrograms of LSD, or 0.2-0.5 grams of mushrooms. The dose is subperceptual – enough to feel a little bit of energy lift, a little bit of insight, but not so much that you are tripping.

Startup founders and executives in Silicon Valley are looking this way for the philosopher's stone that will magically convert their brains into supercharged brains of the members of the cluster of billionaires. They claim that a micro dose of LSD make them feel the flow - a peak performance condition of their brain. They may be not entirely wrong but they are moving in an entirely wrong direction.

Billionaires spend decades in the state of flow without any chemical boosters. The investment of time is not a miracle. It produces much more sustainable outcome than microdosing because it creates a number of very strong positive feedback loops which reinforce physiological changes in their brains and make them difficult to be reversed. It starts from small steps which may easily seem unimportant. Therefore many people chasing their success easily skip them. "Successful people do everything what unsuccessful people don't want to do." Says John Paul DeJoria, the billionaire who slept in his car and sold shampoo door-to-door before he teamed up with Paul Mitchell in 1980 and turned $700 into hair-care outfit John Paul Mitchell Systems. It's a cruel truth for those who are dreaming about consuming billions instead of working on making great products.

When Yuri Milner became my client in 2000 he only began to learn the internet. I failed to deliver him qualified candidates but the dropping NASDAQ saved my ass. However Milner's need for candidates which we failed to deliver didn't evaporate entirely however as did the need of other fresh investors in internet. Then he was not a billionaire but he behaved like one already. He said to me that the right time had come for him to explore the new market without throwing at it a fortune. Candidates' compensations dropped down twofold. So did our fees but we were working when others were just idle. We were moving and everyone wanted to speak to us. That was the Milner's style. It is the style of the cluster of billionaires. Chaos is not a disaster for them. It's a maximization of choices.

Yuri Milner is investing into the right people, not businesses. Being 'right' for Milner doesn't mean to meet some fixed criteria.

He is not a fan of Anna Karenina principle that says that "happy families are all alike; every unhappy family is unhappy in its own way." On the contrary, Milner believes that each founder of a super successful company is different. He gets to know each of the founders he is interested in extremely well. He used to have long walks together with Jan Koum before investing into WhatsApp talking hours about everything except business. He picks founders who look like they will change the world over the next 10 to 20 years. For Milner investing is all about finding the right person that means meeting a lot of people and digging deep with those who seem the right fit. Anyway, the positive outcome is not guaranteed. You can not even hit the target more frequently than to miss it. You need to at least do it sometimes. "That's why investing is so difficult," he says. "Each time it's slightly different. If there was a formula, everyone would be doing it."

Dropoff

"Roustam Tariko, the creator of Russian Standard vodka, became the second vodka producer and distributer in the world after Diageo: in June 2013 he bought stake in Polish CEDC, one of the world's largest vodka producers... He earned his first money in the late 1980s helping foreign tourists find rooms in Moscow hotels... In 1998 he created Russian Standard as Russia's first upscale vodka brand. The following year, with the help of McKinsey & Co., he set up Russian Standard Bank, pioneering in the consumer credit market and becoming the market leader in it three years later... He has villa Minerva on Sardinia, which he bought in 2004 from Silvio Berlusconi's wife for 15 million euro, villa on Miami Beach, which he bought in 2011 for $25.5 million. He has a yacht named after his twin daughters AnnaEva and a Boeing 737 for trips around the world." Forbes 2016 Billionaires List: Dropoff.

"You always have to make an extra effort." Roustam repeated like a mantra when I joined his executive team to execute a major reorganization in his Roust company. It was him, who first explained me the difference between something that matters and other things, which doesn't matter at all. "When you focus on routine tasks which you can easily do, it is not what I am paying you for." He said: "Try and do something that is really hard to accomplish, something that only you can do; just one thing at a time."

It was not easy but it was a real fun. Sometimes. I didn't have passion for vodka. I had passion for people. Our ways with Roustam parted. Not long ago I was fascinated to find almost exactly the same words as Roustam told me long ago in the book "From Zero to One" by Peter Thiel. Thiel recommends in his book to always give people tasks which are unique and which only these particular people can accomplish. One more piece of the puzzle about the habits of the cluster of billionaires was put in place. Tariko and Thiel gave very different explanations why they did it, but it is always the same with the explanations. Look at what they do. Don't listen to what they say. Termites react rather than think but their reactions assemble into a fully rational behavior.

Having billions doesn't make anyone automatically the member of the cluster of billionaires. There are plenty of billionaires who simply inherited their wealth. Some seem to have inherited it from themselves. While regular winning creates a positive feedback loop that enhances mental abilities of the members of the cluster there are also factors which trigger a negative feedback loop that stops their growth, brings them back to normal or even damage their brains. A lasting exposure to the excess of power seems to be the strongest stopping factor. Some just stop running in the self development race. Others switch to a dominance hierarchy related game. There is a chapter in this book about the stopping time and the stopping law. It can be possible that some members of the cluster may neglect a stopping rule while pursuing a secondary goal. Then the secondary goal may eventually substitute the passion (purpose, calling) that is the major driver of their growth. As a result their growth may stop too. Whichever is the reason some members of the cluster stop growing and this way they become heirs of themselves which they used to be as members of the cluster.

Members of the cluster are making billions and use them for achieving goals which are important for them. They do it most visibly when they already have billions but long before that they already start to follow their passion. Members of the cluster like anyone else don't develop their passion. They just have it as most of us do. "You don't choose your passion. A passion chooses you." As Jeff Bezos, the founder of Amazon.com, puts it. Unlike most of us they choose to follow their passion. "People say you have to have a lot of passion to what you are doing. And it's totally true. And the reason is… because it's so hard and if you don't, any rational person would give up." Steve Jobs explained.

An application for bankruptcy by Russian Standard vodka brand owner Roust Corp has been granted by the US Bankruptcy Court on January 9, 2017. According to Roust, the filing was lodged in an attempt to reduce the company's debt by offering bondholders a debt-for-equity swap. Roustam Tariko will continue to own the controlling stake in the reorganised Roust. For some reason these news do not fit with my memories about Roustam when we worked together more than a decade ago. Then Roustam had passion. He was in the cluster. Now, it seems, he is a dropoff not only from the list of Forbes. Further in this book we will see how winning makes our brains better and power is making our brains worse. If your passion is about business your brain will be spoiled by power sooner or later because business is a power play after all. I have learned while writing this book that there are people who still have billions but they are dropping off the cluster of billionaires.

The Longest Dwarf

*"Together with college buddies and fellow billionaires German
Khan and Alexei Kuzmichev, Ukraine native Mikhail Fridman
shares control of Alfa Group, the biggest financial and
industrial investment group in Russia. The trio have been
partners since 1989, when they started commodities trader
Alfa-Eco. Two years later they launched Alfa-Bank, now the
biggest private bank in Russia. The group bought Tyumen Oil
from the state in the late 1990s and merged it with BP's Russian
assets to form TNK-BP. They sold their stakes in the oil giant in
2013." Forbes about #63 in Forbes Billionaires 2016.*

"A financial holding company is looking for a managing director."
Andrey spotted a small ad on the inner back page of the
Kommersant newspaper that he received from a flight attendant
while boarding a Tupolev 154 plane departing from Moscow to
Kiev. He circled out the ad with his pen and put the newspaper
into his briefcase with an intention to call the phone number in
the ad after returning to Moscow two weeks later.

He called the number on his return as planned. A personal
assistant on the other end of the line said to him that the search
was long ago over and the vacancy had been already occupied.
However Andrey managed to talk her into putting him through to
her boss -- Mikhail. After two minutes of talking Mikhail invited
Andrey to the office of the financial holding company -- into a
power substation building hiding in a monstrous housing block
in one of so called 'sleeping' suburbs of Moscow.

"I was curious to meet so young head of the Komsomol
organisation of one of the leading Moscow universities." Mikhail
admitted in their first meeting confirming that the vacancy had

been already filled. However they agreed that Andrey will prepare an investment strategy proposal for Mikhail's financial holding company in a week's time. Andrey had a degree in physics. He never heard about investment industry before. There was no internet in Moscow to look up what the investment strategy was. Andrey as a true scientist went to the public library. In two weeks Mikhail hired Andrey with a mission to build from scratch an investment arm of the financial holding company based on the strategy prepared by him.

Now a quarter of a century later they still work together. For the last decade both have been on the list of Russian billionaires published annually by the Russian Forbes.

Twenty five years ago Andrey had no car and commuted to work by metro. Mikhail often picked him up at the metro station nearest to their power substation office. The founder and the CEO of the financial holding company was already rich then: he owned a rusty Soviet made Lada sedan that he was driving himself. During a five minute drive they managed to discuss their plans for the day. They both behaved then as if they were billionaires. They were investing their time with excellent returns. They already were in the cluster of billionaires.

I first time met Andrey Kosogov in late 1990-s and worked on search assignments for him for a decade. I met Mikhail Fridman only once in 2012 when we had a chance to discuss some of my top level placements with TNK-BP oil giant when he still owned it. "He was a master in talking." Friedman told me about a guy who, I believed, was a real doer. In that conversation with Fridman I realized that the guy whom we discussed had indeed accomplished many things which many people including him and me considered very important but which mattered nothing to the members of the cluster of billionaires; nothing at all.

As I already mentioned before, members of the cluster of billionaires were scarce in Russian large businesses. Perhaps the Alpha Group was the only exception in this regard. Nine people from the Alpha Group already appeared in the list of billionaires in the Russian edition of Forbes as early as 2007. There were one - a maximum of two from any other industrial and investment group. Then I decided that Alpha is a smithy of billionaires. Now I realise that as the PayPal Mafia in Silicon Valley it had become a node in the network of the cluster of billionaires. Moreover, not only the founders in the leadership of Alpha Group, but also executives on the payroll such as Andrey Kosogov and one of the first Russian cosmonauts Alexei Leonov belonged to the cluster. Kosogov became a billionaire. Leonov didn't, but his influence on this node, especially in its formative stage, in many instances, perhaps, even surpassed the influence of Mikhail Friedman. "Friedman was my teacher in business. Leonov - for life. " - Kosogov told me once. "Alpha - this is the longest dwarf." One of the Russian billionaires from the Forbes list said to me, bearing in mind that of all the oligarchic groups, it was the most civilized. I give to this description a very different meaning. Billionaires of Alpha Group were dwarfed by the power that spoiled their brains. Russian business is more about power than any other business in the world. The Alfa Group was the largest Russian node in the network of the cluster of billionaires, but due to the peculiarities of Russian business it didn't create around it a constellation of smaller nodes, as it happened to the PayPal mafia.

Disclaimer

I don't personally know American billionaires like I know some Russian ones. I learned about them from books, publications and interviews. Thanks to YouTube it is not necessary anymore to personally conduct interviews with them. All imaginable questions are asked, answered and recorded on video. You need just to watch and listen.

Why am I writing only about billionaires? According to Malcolm Gladwell there are plenty of outliers among people of other occupations but it is easier for me to write about billionaires. A billion is a good integrated criterion of selection. Furthermore I started my research from business leaders. Thus I leave outstanding scientists, artists, musicians, writers and athletes to Malcolm Gladwell and other writers.

The Mafia Photo

"Peter Thiel has gone from successful entrepreneur to successful venture capitalist. The PayPal cofounder was Facebook's first professional investor, giving Mark Zuckerberg and his hoodied cohorts a $500,000 check in 2004 in return for more than 10% of the company. Thiel still sits on Facebook's board, but sold most of his stake in the Menlo Park, Calif.-based social networking company following its May 2012 IPO. His various venture firms include Founders Fund, which backed rocket builder SpaceX and CIA-backed data-mining software company, Palantir, where he is also a cofounder. FORBES revealed in May 2016 that Thiel was secretly funding the legal costs of Hulk Hogan, a former professional wrestler who sued website Gawker for publishing a sex tape of him with his friend's wife. That lawsuit led to a $140 million verdict in favor of Hogan and set in motion a process that led to Gawker filing for bankruptcy in June 2016. Thiel also supported Donald Trump's 2016 bid for presidency, and was appointed to Trump's transition team following his electoral victory." Forbes, #246, Forbes 400 (2016).

This picture features some of the most poorly dressed men of 2000s: outsized sportswear, leather blazers, and silky shirts. These 13 men are worth billions and billions of dollars. They are the PayPal mafia dressed as gangsters for the 2007 Fortune magazine shoot that gave birth to their famous moniker. In the back row from left we see: Jawed Karim, co-founder Youtube; Jeremy Stoppelman, CEO Yelp; Andrew McCormack, managing partner Laiola Restaurant; Premal Shah, president of Kiva. In the second row from left there are: Luke Nosek, managing partner The Founders Fund; Kenny Howery, managing partner The

Founders Fund; David Sacks, CEO Geni and Room 9 Entertainment; Peter Thiel, CEO Clarium Capital and Founders Fund; Keith Rabois, vice president for business development at Slide and original Youtube investor; Reid Hoffman, founder Linkedin; Max Levchin, CEO Slide; Roelof Botha, partner Sequoia Capital; Russel Simmons, CTO and co-founder of Yelp.

Three key people are missing from the picture. YouTube founders Chad Hurley and Steve Chen were not allowed to participate by the corporate HQ of Google. Elon Musk, founder of Tesla and SpaceX couldn't attend the shot because of a scheduling conflict.

"Elon Musk is trying to redefine transportation on earth and in space. Through Tesla Motors he is aiming to bring fully-electric vehicles to the mass market; at SpaceX he launches satellites and is working to send humans to other planets. It has been a meteoric rise for Musk, as both companies he helped found and still runs have skyrocketed in value and catapulted Musk into the national spotlight. But it hasn't been all smooth sailing... The South African born Musk immigrated to Canada at the age 17 and then to the U.S. as a transfer student to the University of Pennsylvania. He made his first fortune as a cofounder of PayPal." Forbes, #34, Forbes 400 (2016).

PayPal mafia is a one more large node of the network within the cluster of billionaires. The architecture of this network for the time being resembles the scale-free network architecture. It has a relatively small number of large nodes with a lot of both local and long range connections. Smaller nodes have only local connections. Some small nodes eventually grow into the large hub-nodes. Peter Thiel and Reid Hoffman in 2004 invested 500 000 dollars into Facebook then unknown to anybody. Now Facebook is itself growing into a hub-node. It's very immersive to watch a computer simulation of a growing scale-free networks.

As a new hub-node emerges it immediately increases connectivity of several small nodes by connecting to them. Some of small nodes after reaching a certain threshold begin to grow themselves. A few iterations and new hub-nodes pop up. What's next? We will see soon. There is no need to wait for long: the consolidation of the cluster of billionaires is gaining momentum.

An important question remains: How will all these ambitious, strong willed and powerful people avoid or resolve domination conflicts between themselves? In human groups domination conflicts tend to be very difficult to resolve because no one wants to be on the bottom, and few are willing to share the top. Ants once again can give us a behavioural hint.

Shared Dominance

Researchers at North Carolina State University, the University of Oxford and Arizona State University have developed a behavioral model that explains the complexity and diversity of social hierarchies in well-studied Indian jumping ants.

Sometimes, when a colony's queen dies, the female workers engage in duels -- ritual fights without a clear winner and loser -- to establish dominance. Ultimately, a group of workers which took part in such duels become a cadre of worker queens. Scientists called social hierarchy like that a shared dominance hierarchy. In other ant societies despotic hierarchies or linear hierarchies are most common. In a despotic hierarchy, one individual is dominant and all other individuals share the same subordinate status. In a linear hierarchy, there is a clear pecking order: there is a dominant alpha, a beta who is dominant over all but the alpha, a gamma who is dominant over all but the alpha and beta, and so on.

They identified three behaviors related to establishing a hierarchy in an ant colony: biting, in which one ant bites another's head, has a clear winner and loser, with the winner establishing dominance; policing, in which subordinate workers restrain challengers to a dominant individual; and dueling, in which two individuals engage in a martial display with their antennae, but which has no clear loser.

Then researchers created a computer model that allowed them to manipulate all three behaviors in order to see how the behaviors affected the social structure of a colony. They discovered that duelling was actually a winner-winner interaction, that increased the social authority or standing of both participants.

When biting was present, but policing and dueling were absent, the model resulted in a linear hierarchy. When biting and strong policing were present, the model resulted in a despotic hierarchy with a single dominant individual. It was only when biting, policing and winner-winner dueling were all present that the model resulted in a shared dominance hierarchy.

Another group of researchers from University of Colorado Denver monitored thousands of pavement ants engaged in non-lethal fights which looked more like dance offs lasting for 12-14 hours. It's a huge amount of time. It's still not clear why pavement ants prefer to spend it on dancing instead of foraging but it looks like a yet another example of winner-winner activities.

Yet another group of researchers from North Carolina State University, Arizona State University and the U.S. Department of Agriculture proved that the raise of dopamine levels of Indian jumping ants involved in winner-winner dueling triggered dramatic physical changes in the ants without affecting their DNA. This has made them a model organism for epigenetics researchers. By the way, their life expectancy, for instance, jumped from about six months to several years or more.

Let's leave ants for a moment and look if humans can demonstrate a similar winner-winner behavior.

"Unless they invest in the difficult task of creating new things, American companies will fail in the future no matter how big their profits remain today. What happens when we've gained everything to be had from fine-tuning the old lines of business that we've inherited? Unlikely as it sounds, the answer threatens to be far worse than the crisis of 2008. Today's "best practices" lead to dead ends; the best paths are new and untried." Peter

Thiel writes in his book "Zero to One." There he presents the idea that the traditional market competition is bad for business and economy because its winner-loser model finally leads to a situation in which everybody loses. He offers the model of a creative monopoly instead. "But the world we live in is dynamic: it's possible to invent new and better things. Creative monopolists give customers more choices by adding entirely new categories of abundance to the world. Creative monopolies aren't just good for the rest of society; they're powerful engines for making it better." He writes. Doesn't it sound like an invitation to a winner-winner dance? By focusing on creating abundant resources instead of fighting for the scarce ones the members of the cluster of billionaires engage themselves in a sort of ritual fights without a clear winner and loser.

Please, don't mix the winner-winner duel with the win-win concepts of all sorts presented in the management and personal development literature. A winner-winner fight is not about finding a common ground or a mutually beneficial interest. It's a fight against a difficult problem that the vast majority of people even don't dare trying to resolve.

"Not Less We Praise in Sterner Days"

Eli Goldratt, a business guru who successfully applied methods of physics to social life, wrote his last book "The Choice" in the form of a dialogue between him and his daughter. It starts with a question why Goldratt doesn't feel disappointed with failure. He explains: "Let's suppose that you are a scientist and you are trying to build an instrument that is based on a new approach. Of course, you... will first build a prototype... What would you expect from the prototype?" His daughter answers: "Even if the prototype as an instrument didn't work, as long as it provided new knowledge of which cause-and-effect are valid and which are not, the satisfaction of making progress compensates for the disappointment."

The point is not about the ability to withstand the feeling of disappointment but of the ability to feel more satisfaction than disappointment from failure. The approach of a true scientist proposed by Eli Goldratt differs from the approach of a consumer. A true scientist understands how the instrument works and his aim is to make it working better. A consumer just sees a box and expects that it should work in a certain way. If the box doesn't work or works poorly, a consumer gets disappointed and frustrated. For a true scientist, or in our case a true member of the cluster of billionaires, there is no time for disappointment because a true member of the cluster really sees an opportunity in every problem.

"It's very important to actively seek out and listen very carefully to negative feedback." Elon Musk says in an interview with Foundation 20. He doesn't even think about bad feelings that negative feedback may provoke. He simply doesn't think this way.

"I have obtained the Head Master's permission to alter darker to sterner. "Not less we praise in sterner days." Do not let us speak of darker days: let us speak rather of sterner days. These are not dark days; these are great days - the greatest days our country has ever lived; and we must all thank God that we have been allowed, each of us according to our stations, to play a part in making these days memorable in the history of our race." Sir Winston Churchill said to students of Harrow School on October 28, 1941. It sounds like he had a true scientist's (or the cluster of billionaires) approach, hadn't he?

Winning is a Drug

"Winning is not a sometime thing; it's an all the time thing. You don't win once in a while; you don't do things right once in a while; you do them right all of the time. Winning is a habit. Unfortunately, so is losing." Vincent T. Lombardi said. He was the greatest legendary football coach of his time, and his unique approach to teaching, motivating and inspiring players not only turned the Green Bay Packers into the most dominating NFL team in the 1960s, but also influenced the most prominent leaders in business for decades.

Vince Lombardy, when he said the above, was not, of course, aware of the findings of neuroscientists which occurred long after his death. Ian Robertson, Professor of Psychology at Trinity College Dublin, in his book "The Winner Effect" claims that a dopamine jump in the brain after winning has an effect of a strong drug, that makes people more focused, smarter, more confident and more aggressive. For this reason according to Robertson the more winners win, the more they go on winning. "Success has powerful effects on the brain: it increases levels of the hormone testosterone in both men and women, and ramps up the brain's chemical messenger dopamine's activity." Roberson writes in his blog. "Success also acts like a tranquilliser – it reduces levels of the stress-hormone cortisol – and may even have mild anti-depressant qualities. Finally, its psychological effects are powerful – it gives our self-confidence and feeling of control over the world an ego-enhancing boost."

The downside is that winning in the winner-loser models of dominance hierarchies always leads to the winner getting more powerful. Even small, experimentally induced power levels increase hypocrisy, moral exceptionalism, egocentricity and lack of empathy for others. Large doses of power become destructive especially for individuals who are prone to the need for power.

The shared dominance hierarchy that emerges from the winner-winner duelling of the members of the cluster of billionaires may well help them be less prone to the downside impact of power.

As we saw before, the uniqueness of the goal of each cluster representative makes their competition unique as they each fight not against each other but to create and offer a genuinely unique solution to a truly hard and unique problem. What about their team working within one project or one company?

Like a pair of lovers, members of the cluster choose each other for working together mutually. "So we set out to hire people who would actually enjoy working together. They had to be talented, but even more than that they had to be excited about working specifically with us." Peter Thiel writes. It's purely pragmatic approach.

Humans independently of their age and experience tend to be bad at evaluating other humans. Typically, we make mistake in 50% of our people choices. I met executives and businessmen, which claimed that their success rate was close to 75%. Those, who attributed so high success to their own knowledge of human nature with time proved to be accomplished power seekers who just overestimated their own capabilities. The real success rate of these people in hiring others was close to zero. Just a few like Peter Thiel tried hard to figure out not only if they liked a candidate, but also to understand and feel if the candidate really liked them. By doing so they dramatically increase the probability of their successful work together. They also focus their efforts on winner-winner fight for achieving the common goal instead of internal fights and policing. "The best thing I did as a manager at PayPal was to make every person in the company responsible for doing just one thing. Every employee's one thing was unique, and everyone knew I would evaluate him only on that one thing. I had started doing this just to simplify the task of managing people. But then I noticed a deeper result: defining roles reduced conflict." Thiel writes.

Deliberate Practice

The book "Peak" authored by Anders Ericsson, Professor of Psychology at Florida State University was published in summer of 2016. Ericsson tries to clarify in this book the true meaning of deliberate practice that was coined by Ericsson but popularized and according to Ericsson oversimplified by Malcolm Gladwell under the name "10,000 hour rule" in his book "Outliers" that I already mentioned in this book. "Gladwell didn't distinguish between the type of practice that the musicians in our study did — a very specific sort of practice referred to as "deliberate practice" which involves constantly pushing oneself beyond one's comfort zone, following training activities designed by an expert to develop specific abilities, and using feedback to identify weaknesses and work on them — and any sort of activity that might be labeled "practice." Ericsson says.

Ericsson is skeptical about the influence of genetic differences in cognitive or physical abilities on variations in achievements. In "Peak," he cites a study by British researchers, which found that IQ does indeed predict chess skill among children. But when those researchers looked only at kids who were elite chess players, a higher IQ was, in fact, linked to worse performance.

While a higher IQ helps some kids learn the game and acquire the basic skills required to play quicker, once other kids catch up with them, intelligence level probably doesn't matter, Ericsson explains. But deliberate practice does.

I think that the concept of deliberate practice that recently has come under intense scrutiny from other psychologists is far from universal. It overlaps however to certain extent with the special treatment of time that enables members of the cluster of billionaires to turbocharge their brains to the very peak of performance. Let's start with the first principle, first, before digging into the complicated matter of time.

Ab Initio

"You just have to be born a genius."

"No, you don't. I was not born with any exceptional brainpower, and I have my IQ results from my youth to confirm it. I am a bodybuilder. Practice. Practice. Practice. Efrat, when you will realize that you, like any other person, have enough intuition and brainpower to think like a true scientist?"

From "The Choice" by Eliyahu Goldratt

Eliyahu Goldratt was a scientist in physics before becoming a guru in management. He knew what he was talking about. Elon Musk is an entrepreneur that doesn't prevent him from following the advice of Goldratt.

"I think it's important to reason from first principles rather than by analogy," Elon Musk said in an interview with Kevin Rose. "The normal way we conduct our lives is we reason by analogy. We are doing this because it's like something else that was done, or it is like what other people are doing. It's kind of mentally easier to reason by analogy than from first principle. But first principle is a kind of physics way of looking at the world. And what it really means is that you kind of boil things down to the most fundamental truths ... and reason up from there. That takes a lot more mental energy."

According to Cambridge Dictionary first principle is "the basic and most important reasons for doing or believing something." In physics, a calculation is said to be from the first principles, or ab initio, if it starts directly at the level of established laws of physics. Over 2300 years ago, Aristotle said that a first principle is the "first basis from which a thing is known." Richard

Feynman, a Nobel Prize winning physicist, explained this approach to his students in more simple words: don't try to remember; try to understand and if you understand the subject deep enough you will remember it automatically.

Musk believes that first principle is the only right approach when you want to do something new. It's mentally hard and counterintuitive but it is the only thing that works. You can see that his views are very much in line with Peter Thiel's concept of creative monopoly. They use different words but they speak about the same thing, don't they?

Digging deep down to the root of the subject doesn't only create the ultimate understanding necessary to change or improve it but it also helps the members of the cluster of billionaires to faster develop a deep understanding of other subjects. They achieve it by unconsciously applying the method of learning transfer.

Learning Transfer

Learning transfer is a process when we use our existing knowledge to help us to learn entirely new things. There is no secret in learning transfer as in any other practices of the members of the cluster of billionaires. It doesn't promise huge results from the beginning because it's another exponential practice that starts with obtaining of in-depth -- down to first principle -- understanding of just one subject. This first step requires huge efforts and plenty of time but provides very moderate results. Next step is faster. Another even more faster. It's still hard but understanding of a difficult problem brings joy. A positive feedback loop starts working.

Researchers have identified some key characteristics of learning transfer:

1. All new learning involves transfer based on previous learning. We all use our already obtained knowledge and our past learning experience in the process of learning new things.

2. Initial learning is necessary for transfer. If we didn't learn anything before, we have nothing to transfer.

3. Knowledge that is overly contextualized can reduce transfer; abstract representations of knowledge can help promote transfer. This point is key. If you understand one thing in principle, you can look at the other thing and see something similar to your understanding, again, in principle. If you remember only details, your knowledge will be useless because a sum of details will not give you understanding.

4. Transfer is an active, dynamic process rather than a passive end-product of a particular set of learning experiences. It means

you can learn by transfer several things simultaneously, especially when your brain cognitive performance will grow dramatically.

Investors of Time

What billionaires value most? Exactly! Time. Money is not a scarce resource for billionaires but time is flowing for them as it is for all people. No one can move against the arrow of time. Entropic barrier is too high.

Time can be saved, but saving it is a boring and tedious process that prevents a person from enjoying its each moment. A time lived without joy is the time lost in vain. Everyone -- and billionaires too -- have unpleasant, difficult and meaningless moments. The reasons for their occurrence is out of our control. Saving time, striving to accomplish as much as possible at the expense of sensing the uniqueness of our each experienced moment - it's a waste of time that we are able to prevent. You invest time if you enjoy doing the right things.

The members of the cluster of billionaires value time, but they do it differently from what is written in the books on time management. As they often do with problems that can't be solved by optimization, they reframe the problem: you shouldn't manage time; you should invest it. "I do not care what you're going to do, if you think about our challenges 24 hours 7 days a week." - Roustam Tariko used to tell me. What he had in mind was not thinking, as such, but a particular brain activity when it constantly asks itself questions: "What do I know? What I do not know? "Depending on the answer it treats familiar problems subconsciously, and focuses consciousness on unfamiliar problems.

"Don't be trapped by dogma, which is living with the results of other people's thinking." Steve Jobs said in his famous Stanford commencement speech. "Think differently!" Was a slogan of one of the most successful Apple's advertising campaigns. The ability of reframing a problem goes hand in hand with a habit of thinking differently. It helps to find an entirely new radical solution to a problem instead of wasting time on incremental improvements.

Here we have to go back to the concept of radical plasticity of the brain. The second order network that is responsible for metacognition in addition to the same sensory and memory information that is used by the first order network uses also some other information. Scientists don't know the source of that information so far. The brain runs in parallel multiple subconscious processes. The beam of consciousness moves as LIDAR from one process to the other, tracing the contours of the surrounding reality. Algorithms that lead to success, get remembered. Errors are analyzed and bring a lot of useful information. Books read open the way of thinking of their authors. Events are experienced repeatedly and discussed from different perspectives. Time gets compressed. Steve Jobs was said to create a "reality distortion field". This expression is usually used as a metaphor to emphasize the charisma of Steve and his ability to convince . In reality his field actually distorted reality because time inside that field flowed with different speed than outside it.

Fernand Braudel, one of the most important historians of the 20th century, in his book On History in 1950 introduced a then revolutionary conception of historical time. History in geographical, social and individual times introduced by Bradel has a different speed in each of them. In geographical time the history of man and his surroundings "unfolds slowly and is slow to alter, often repeating itself and working itself out in cycles which are endlessly renewed." Social time refers to "history of gentle rhythms, of groups and groupings" which Braudel compares to "deeply running currents." Individual time is history on the scale "of men in particular." This "surface disturbance" Braudel finds "most exciting and richest in human interest of histories."

Existence of multiple time scales later was recognized in biology, chemistry and physics. We can illustrate it with the following example on the microscopic level: on one scale, atoms vibrate with a frequency of approx. 10^{13} 1/s, on the other scale, phenomena and applications of practical interest occur on a timescale of seconds.

Our personal time can also move with different speed. We all experience time flying or crawling. Michael Flaherty, Professor of Sociology in Eckerd College explains this paradox with the density of experience per standard temporal unit. "From the standpoint of a clock or calendar, each standard temporal unit is exactly the same: Every minute contains 60 seconds; every day contains 24 hours. However, standard temporal units vary in what I've dubbed "the density of human experience" – the volume of objective and subjective information they carry...We pay increased attention to strange circumstances," he writes, "which amplifies the density of experience per standard temporal unit – and time, in turn, seems to pass slowly."

I guess, his explanation gives us the key to the understanding of how the members of the cluster of billionaires compress their time -- they amplify the density of their experience per standard temporal unit by thinking differently, by reframing problems, by using the first principle, by building creative monopolies. Passion adds to the volume of information that each moment of life -- or each standard temporal unit carry. The cluster of billionaires has its own scale of time that compresses into seconds the volume of information that people outside the cluster are stretching for years.

If we forget for a while about seconds, hours, years and other standard temporal units we will see that individual time of each of us has a different speed. Even for the same person the speed of time varies depending on the intensity of information inflow that the person receives on a given moment. Intensity of information inflow depends on the importance of information, on one hand, and on its volume, on the other. Volume matters nothing without importance because our consciousness simply ignore unimportant information. The information may come from the outside -- from our senses -- and from the inside -- from our memory and thinking. The members of the cluster of billionaires constantly secure both high importance and big volume of their information inflow.

Passion? Calling! Purpose! Passion!

"People say: you have to have a lot of passion for what you are doing. And it's totally true. And the reason is: because it's so hard that if you don't any rational person would give up. It's really hard. And you have to do it over a sustained period of time. So if you don't love it, if you don't have fun doing it, if you don't really love it, you gonna give up." Steve Jobs said on May 30, 2007 at D 5 conference. It is, probably, the best ever description of one of the most basic principles of the cluster: You have to really love what you are doing.

Elon Musk adds to the above that if you love what you are doing you are thinking about it all the time. "I didn't go into the rocket business, the car business or the solar business thinking this is a great opportunity," Musk told Steven Kotler, bestselling co-author of Abundance and Bold, in an interview. "I just thought, in order to make a difference, something needed to be done. I wanted to have an impact. I wanted to create something substantially better than what came before."

Peter Thiel is reframing the definition of the driving force of the members of the cluster to better reflect its strong linking to the real world: "To follow your calling is something much better than just doing something you are passionate about. Passion is more about the interior state of mind... It is about doing something that is important and that nobody else can do; about doing good things... Framing of the question in the larger context of our world is always worth thinking about."

According to Peter Thiel, passion in the cluster is not about being passionate about something; it's about having a calling to do something meaningful.

"If you have internally this burning need to do something, push yourself, you are also doing yourself a disservice by not serving this need." Says WeWork co-founder, Miguel McKelvey in an interview with Entrepreneur Network partner Bryan Elliott. "Because then you are not following you true path. And that's not right for you either. It gonna be doing some damage to your psyche if like everyday something is telling you: 'Take action. Move forward. Do something.' And instead... you are just checking in a box or punching a timecard whatever."

Pursuit of Happiness

"Twenty-three hundred years ago Aristotle concluded that, more than anything else, men and women seek happiness. While happiness itself is sought for its own sake, every other goal—health, beauty, money, or power—is valued only because we expect that it will make us happy. Much has changed since Aristotle's time. Our understanding of the worlds of stars and of atoms has expanded beyond belief. The gods of the Greeks were like helpless children compared to humankind today and the powers we now master. And yet on this most important issue very little has changed in the intervening centuries. We do not understand what happiness is any better than Aristotle did, and as for learning how to attain that blessed condition, one could argue that we have made no progress at all." Mihaly Csikszentmihalyi wrote in his book "Flow: The Psychology of Optimal Experience" more than a quarter of a century ago. He is today Claremont Graduate University's Distinguished Professor of Psychology and Management. He is also the founder and co-director of the Quality of Life Research Center -- a nonprofit research institute that studies positive psychology, the study of human strengths such as optimism, creativity, intrinsic motivation, and responsibility.

Mihaly Csikszentmihalyi starts his book with the notion of happiness because he has concluded that "flow" is the state of happiness. According to him flow is a condition "when the information that keeps coming into awareness is congruent with goals, psychic energy flows effortlessly. There is no need to worry, no reason to question one's adequacy. But whenever one does stop to think about oneself, the evidence is encouraging: "You are doing all right." The positive feedback strengthens the self, and more attention is freed to deal with the outer and the inner environment." 'In the zone' is another term for flow popular among athletes.

Let's examine next what happens with time when athletes are "in the zone."

In the Zone

Back in 1999, Sue Jackson and Mihaly Csikszentmihalyi authored a book titled, "Flow in Sports: The Keys to Optimal Experiences and Performances." Still relevant today, this book highlights ten common elements which athletes experience during optimal performances.

In the zone the athlete's sense of time changes. Some athletes have indicated that their performances seem to happen very quickly, almost as if they can't believe it when it's over, while others say time moves in slow motion. During these slower motion experiences, athletes report seeming to have more time to hit a fastball, shoot a 3-pointer, or move through traffic during a race. Time becomes flexible in the zone. It can be experienced as both very fast and very slow as if an athlete can use 'fast forward' and 'slow play' buttons to regulate the speed of time. Standard temporal units have nothing to do with this phenomena. The radical plasticity of brains, probably, does.

The cluster of billionaires does the same with the sense of time of its members what the zone does for athletes but it has a much more lasting effect because it involves the radical plasticity that makes their brains perform differently all the time not just sometimes.

"To Strive, to Seek, to Find, and not to Yield"

In March 2011 the final line of Alfred Tennyson's poem 'Ulysses' – 'To strive, to seek, to find, and not to yield' – was selected as the inscription for a wall in the athlete's village at the 2012 London Olympic Games. But there was a danger that the adoption of the line as a monumental pronouncement of optimism, isolated from its context within the poem as a whole, might threaten to rob Tennyson's poetry of its nuance. This danger was lessened, however, by the subsequent decision to lengthen the inscription to incorporate the final three-and-a-half lines of Ulysses' monologue:

"That which we are, we are;

One equal temper of heroic hearts,

Made weak by time and fate, but strong in will

To strive, to seek, to find, and not to yield."

However affirmative and persuasive the poem's final lines might be, they are also full of doubt and equivocation. As Tennyson himself suggested, confidence and doubt are equal elements of his poem's meaning: he said that it 'was written under the sense of loss and that all had gone by, but that still life must be fought out to the end'.

These lines with all their ambivalence might well become the motto of the cluster of billionaires because the cognition of the members of the cluster is not distorted by the loss aversion cognitive bias coined by Daniel Kahneman, a professor of behavioral & cognitive psychology at Princeton, winner of the

2002 Nobel Prize for economics, and author of the best-selling book on cognitive biases and heuristics: Thinking Fast & Slow.

"Losses loom larger than gains. And we have a pretty good idea of by how much they loom larger than gains, and it's by about 2-to-1." Kahneman explains in an "Masters in Business" podcast with Barry Ritholtz. "An example is: I'll offer you a gamble on the toss of a coin. If it shows tails, you lose $100. And if it shows heads, you win X. What would X have to be for that gamble to become really attractive to you? Most people – and this has been well established – demand more than $200... Meaning it takes $200 of potential gain to compensate for $100 of potential loss when the chances of the two are equal. So that's loss aversion. It turns out that loss aversion has enormous consequences."

New challenges are for the members of the cluster investments of time, opening new experiences and opportunities. As I mentioned before, they don't have the loss aversion cognitive bias that is typical for people from the cluster of consumers. "I had a lot of joint projects of McKinsey." Roustam Tariko, the founder of Russian Standard bank and vodka brand once said in my presence to Vladimir Melnikov, the founder of the giant apparel company Gloria Jeans. "Half of them ended in failure. But the other half generated profits, which are by orders of magnitude bigger than losses from failures. " This simple phrase comprises a whole bunch of approaches typical to the members of the cluster of billionaires. First, they always act in the face of uncertainty. Secondly, they focus on success rather than failure. Third, they assess the probability and make decisions, understanding risk and accepting it.

"If I go do this thing, that I genuinely believe is gonna be a big deal and I fail, am I gonna regret having tried and failed? The answer then was no. But I knew that I would always regret it if I didn't try." Jeff Bezos recalled his thoughts when he made the decision to quit a prominent Wall Street firm and to start the Amazon.com.

Again, it is easier for them to take risks, because failure for them is also the investment of time. Trial and error for them is a method to learn the world with the highest return on investment of their time.

"Screw It, Let's Do It"

"One of Britain's highest-profile billionaires, Richard Branson owes his fortune to a conglomerate of businesses bearing the Virgin brand, many of which he no longer controls. Among his more famous exits: the sale of Virgin Records for $1 billion in 1992, which reportedly made Branson run down London's Ladbroke Grove crying." Forbes about # 286 Billionaires (2016).

I used one of Richard Branson's favourite sayings and the title of his book as the heading of this chapter because it may become the motto of all self made billionaires. Sir Richard placed at his page at Virgin.com a quote from Dale Carnegie, author of books How to Stop Worrying and Start Living and How to Win Friends and Influence People with a comment that made his attitude towards action absolutely clear: "He said "Inaction breeds doubt and fear. Action breeds confidence and courage. If you want to conquer fear, do not sit home and think about it. Go out and get busy." Dale was absolutely right. The more you do something, the more you grow in confidence and expertise."

"You are better off trying to do something that does not work and learning from that instead of not doing anything at all." Mark Zuckerberg, the founder and CEO of Facebook starts. "You can't be only a person who just talks and talks, and talks. You have to actually go and do something." Jimmy Wales, the founder of Wikipedia continues.

Action is the way how members of the cluster explore their path. With each step they learn new things which help them to better predict the future. I am tempted to put here a lot more quotes like the above but I hope there are already enough for you to believe them and me. If you don't know what to do, do something about it, seriously. Now it's time for a bit of theory.

Action is, probably, the first principle of the cluster of billionaires if this action is taken to move ahead on their way to their purpose when they follow their passion and their calling. Action means taking risks especially if you are doing something entirely new but members of the cluster of billionaires tacitly know one very important secret: stability is an illusion.

David Meets Goliath

The Biblical fight between David and Goliath provides a very good example of the difference between the probabilistic approach of the members of the cluster of billionaires, and deterministic views which still dominate the majority of earthlings. It is said in the canonical Bible texts (which are the source of modern memes) that David hurled a stone from his sling with all his might and hit Goliath in the center of his forehead so powerfully, that the stone sank into Goliath's forehead. Goliath fell on his face to the ground, and David cut off his head. It means that David won due to his physical might and agility, which proved to be extraordinary for such a young, subtle and inexperienced person as he was (David was not serving in the army of israelites - he only brought some food to his elder brothers).

The analysis of ancient hebrew texts, however, suggests that canonical reconstructed texts replaced the word mitzchat that meant greaves - the leg armour - with a very similar word meitzach that meant forehead, that was, by the way, protected in Goliath's case with a bronze helmet. The original story said that the stone from David's sling accidentally sank between greaves and the leg of Goliath who bent his leg moving towards David. The giant couldn't straighten his leg and fell, and David cut his throat.

Thus, it turns out that the feat of David was in his willingness to confront the enemy who was much stronger than him while king Saul was hesitating and his soldiers were reluctant to act too as they saw the indecisiveness of their king. David hadn't any special combat skills and he won because of luck (miracle).

The original story tells us that willingness to act and believing in miracles are the most important factors of winning. The later Bible interpretations tells us that the calculation - counting on a physical advantage - is the most important.

David from the original story volunteered to fight without counting on anything because only an idiot could count on something in his situation. He was driven by the need of action and his faith in miracle (luck, God). David from the Bible was counting on his physical advantage already when he volunteered to fight. Just look how the new reading has changed the position requirements for the king! The whole story, you know, was intended to show that David was more suitable for the king's position than Saul.

The need to calculate everything is a typical feature of the brave new world built by our civilization. As you see from the example above the process of making robots out of people was started already by the writers of the Bible. The members of the cluster of billionaires, by the way, are very pragmatic and can calculate well when they deal with situations in which it is easy to calculate the profit irrespectively on the value of a deal. For this reason sometimes they may seem to us petty and materialistic. They suddenly become careless and naive even when the stakes are extremely high but only if the result can not be predicted or calculated. We, the modern humans, very often have the illusion that the result can be accurately predicted in such situations even though it is impossible to predict. We waste tons of time and energy on the attempts to predict unpredictable because we see the stakes to be too high to rely purely on chance. Planning and calculations help members of the cluster of billionaires to deal with uncertainty because they apply them adequately. They use the synthesis of the two approaches - calculating/ planning and taking chances - instead of choosing between them.

God Does not Play Dice, Billionaires Do

"Amazon's chief Jeff Bezos added $20 billion to his net worth over 14 months through December 2016, the largest gain of anyone in the world. The online retailer's stock shares soared thanks in part to its booming cloud-computing unit, Amazon Web Services. Bezos boasted at the 2016 shareholders meeting that Amazon is the fastest company ever to reach $100 billion in annual sales, which it cleared in 2015. Big gains often come from taking bold risks. "We are the best place in the world to fail (we have plenty of practice!), and failure and invention are inseparable twins," Bezos wrote in his last annual report."
Forbes, #2, Forbes 400 (2016).

Without knowing it, the scientist in the field of thermodynamics formulated the secret of success of the members of the cluster of billionaires: they base their decisions on the probability calculus. Most of them do not know this secret themselves, as long as you do not tell them. They simply live that way. Perhaps, they are one of the ways of nature to create order out of chaos.

Jeff Bezos demonstrates his probabilistic thinking very well when he tells the story of how he spoke his parents into investing into his startup venture: "I told them there was 70% chance they would lose their entire investment. And that was an important disclosure for me because I wanted to be able to go home for thanksgiving dinner no matter what happened."

"If you are ready to take bold bets there gonna be experiments. And in experiments you don't know ahead of time if it's gonna work. Experiments are by their very nature prone to failure but a few big successes compensate for dozens and dozens of things that didn't work." Bezos says.

"Failure is always interesting to talk about in a sense that for some people it seems like a finish line and for other people it's a point to spring forward from." WeWork co-founder, Miguel McKelvey continues the thought of Bezos.

"Miguel McKelvey is the other half of WeWork, the nearly $17 billion communal work space company, cofounded in 2010 with CEO Adam Neumann. Raised in a five-mother commune in Eugene, Ore., McKelvey now serves as Chief Creative Officer, directing construction, architecture and web design for the business that has raised more than $1 billion from investors like Goldman Sachs, JP Morgan Chase, and Benchmark Capital. WeWork, which now rents out offices in over 30 cities around the world, touts perks like arcade rooms and on-site beer kegs, and also provides computing services and access to health insurance." Forbes, 2017

"Einstein's saying, "God does not play dice," is well known. In the same spirit Poincare stated that for a supreme mathematician there is no place for probabilities. However, Poincare himself mapped the path leading to the answer to this problem. He noticed that when we throw dice and use probability calculus, it does not mean that we suppose dynamics to be wrong. It means something quite different. We apply the probability concept because in each interval of initial conditions, however small, there are as "many" trajectories that lead to each of the faces of the dice. This is precisely what happens with unstable dynamic systems." Nobel prize laureate in thermophysics Ilya Prigogine and his colleague Isabelle Stengers wrote in their groundbreaking book 'Order out of Chaos'. "God could, if he wished to, calculate the trajectories in an unstable dynamic world. He would obtain the same result as probability calculus permits us to reach." Without knowing it, scientists in the field of thermodynamics formulated the secret of success of the members of the cluster of billionaires: they base their decisions on the probability calculus. Most of them do not know this secret themselves, as long as you do not tell them. They simply live that way. Perhaps, they are one of the ways of nature to create order out of chaos.

Monty Hall Problem

The Monty Hall Problem is a probability puzzle that is based on the American television game show Let's Make a Deal and named after its original host, Monty Hall.

There are 3 doors, behind which there are two goats and a car. You pick a door (call it door A). You're hoping for the car of course. Monty Hall examines the other doors (B & C) and always opens one of them with a goat. If both doors have goats he'll randomly pick one to open.

Now you can either stick with your original pick - door A (original guess) or switch to the other unopened door. What would you prefer?

Common sense tells you that the chances are 50-50 but in reality if you switch the door your chances to win will become 2/3.

The explanation is pretty simple. When you pick one door out of three the probability of you choosing the right door with a car behind it is 1/3. Right? After the door with a goat behind it has been opened the probability of a car being behind the unpicked door remains 2/3. Still looks weird, isn't it?

Let's imagine that you have picked one door out of 100 and Monty opens 98 doors with goats behind them from remaining 99 doors.

Will you want a door randomly chosen out of 100 or the best choice out of 99?

Monty is letting us choose between a generic, random choice and a curated, filtered choice. Filtered choice is better.

The Monty Hall Problem puzzle is counter intuitive because we naturally assume that having two choices automatically means having 50-50 chances. Indeed, two choices are equally likely when you know nothing about either choice. If we know that the filter was applied to one of choices then probabilities change. Got it?

Congratulations! You've just learned about the Bayesian filter. Members of the cluster of billionaires intuitively use this counter intuitive approach.

Bayesian Probabilities

Sorry, but we need to dig a little bit into the theory to be able to understand why the time in the cluster of billionaires is not moving with the same speed as the time in the cluster of consumers. There are plenty of theorems and mathematical calculations behind the concepts of Bayesian probabilities, Markov process and others, which we omit here because we are more interested in the general, almost metaphorical application of their basic principles. It is also interesting to see how the practices in the cluster of billionaires are aligned with the advances in science.

In 1770s, Thomas Bayes introduced 'Bayes Theorem'. Now, centuries later, the importance of Bayesian probabilities is just growing. Bayesian probabilities could be thought of as gambling attitudes for placing bets on outcomes. These attitudes are updated always as new data come to light. Members of the cluster of billionaires may even not know about bayesian probabilities. They just live according to them at the same time when the rest of the world continues to follow more intuitive frequentist approach.

Time's arrow emerges together with randomness. Randomness means the lack of predictability. Individual random events are by definition unpredictable. Yet we have probability to deal with unpredictability. There are different probabilistic approaches: frequentist and Bayesian. Let's take a single event with two possible outcomes, say, coin tossing. We can try to predict the probability of future outcomes based on the information of how frequently either outcome occurred before.

Traditional frequentist statistics will first test how many times heads will turn out by repeating the coin tossing for a fixed amount of tries or until another predetermined ending event occurs. Based on outcomes obtained from this sampling experiment it calculates the future probability of heads turning out in coin tossing repeated under the same conditions for an indefinite amount of tries. Same conditions are the key. In other words frequentist approach tries to predict probability of future results on the basis of previous results. It uses old data. That approach works, let me repeat once again, only if the conditions remain the same. For instance, if we are trying to estimate the fairness of tossing a coin, we assume that the same coin will be tossed by the same hand always. If we change the coin or the hand the old data becomes irrelevant.

Bayesian statistics provides people the tools to update their beliefs in the evidence of new data. Without going into too much theory or mathematics we can assume that bayesian probability takes our current beliefs and multiplies them by the parameters, which influence our belief. If either belief or parameters change so does the probability of the event in question.

Time's arrow emerges out of a loss of information. It always points in the direction in which information is lost and can never be retrieved. The information from the past deteriorates and lose its predictive power faster that the information from the present. It is an important principle of the cluster of billionaires. It is known in science as Markov process.

Markov Process

"Andrey Markov was born on 14 June 1856 in Russia. He attended St. Petersburg Grammar. Some teachers saw him as a rebellious student. He performed poorly in most subjects other than mathematics. After the graduation from St. Petersburg university he stayed there to continue his career as a mathematician. He is best known for his work on stochastic processes. A primary subject of his research later became known as Markov chains and Markov processes. Markov chains have many applications as statistical models of real-world processes, such as studying cruise control systems in motor vehicles, queues or lines of customers arriving at an airport, exchange rates of currencies, storage systems such as dams, and population growths of certain animal species. The algorithm known as PageRank, which was originally proposed for the internet search engine Google, is based on a Markov process. Furthermore, Markov processes are the basis for general stochastic simulation methods known as Gibbs sampling and Markov Chain Monte Carlo and have found extensive application in Bayesian statistics."

I guess, the above clarification from Wikipedia doesn't make a Markov process any clearer as it contains too many specific professional terms in itself. Members of the cluster of billionaires apply its principles intuitively. We need to know a bit more theory if we want to understand why what they do is working.

In a Markov process the future is independent of the past, if the present is defined. By defining the present as clearly as they can members of the cluster of billionaires can not only predict future outcomes of their actions with more accuracy but they also can influence the outcomes by increasing their chances for making the right choice. By digging down to the first principle they create a better framework for taking into account as many parameters which influence the future outcome as they can.

Rapid selection of parameters which really matter allows them to make decisions about the future faster without loosing in accuracy. In fact, they are adding more accuracy instead. They achieve it by iterations, by taking steps to influence the parameters which really matter and by recalculating the probability of achieving the next micro target. They are slicing their targets to make sure that the chances to achieve the next target are not less favourable than 50-50.

Following their example we can imagine the future as a number of transparent choice layers. We can pick up layer by layer but in our need to predict the future we can pick up several layers at the same time and try to take our decision based on the probability of the ultimate outcome of a number of choices. In other words we can make choices in each layer consecutively or we can try to make a one time choice about several layers of choice.

For instance, when David from the biblical story about David and Goliath was taking decision if he should volunteer to fight with Goliath who was much bigger and stronger he could make the decision based on two layers. First he had to choose if he should volunteer or not with the probability of 50-50. Second he had to evaluate the probability of him winning against Goliath. The first layer of choice was entirely in his control. By choosing not to fight he would eliminate the opportunity to win entirely. So by volunteering he eliminated on door with a goat behind it. Of course, his choice was more complicated than the Monty Hall Problem because together with increasing his chances to win he was also increasing his chances to die with his first move. Yet with the next layer - his next move - when he hurled a stone out of his sling David already started to increase his chances of winning against his chances of death. It was not a huge increase but it created another window of opportunity for the uncertainty or God, as bible prefers to put it, to interfere with the fight in David's favour.

When David had to decide about fighting with Goliath he already had all information on the worst case scenario. The Goliath's chances to win were already very well filtered based on his previous fights. No new information could make David's chances worse. It could only make his chances better or leave them the same. If you let the uncertainty in and give it the probability of changing the status quo of 50% for each iteration (or each probability layer) you start increasing your chances against the best filtered odds with each iteration.

Some scientists claim that we are not actually making any predictions of the future because we have memory of the future instead. Memory of the future is the full knowledge of the future state of the system based on its current state. Uncertainty, however, spoils this perfect memory by interfering with the causal chain of events somewhere between the present time and the point in time when the 'remembered' event should occur in the future. Therefore our memory of the future should be fine tuned all the time to reflect unexpected interferences. Like with the memory of the past we 'remember' more close events in the future better than more remote. We can also train our memory of the future to be more sensitive to interferences of uncertainty with the causal course of events. It can be yet another explanation of the way how the brains of the members of the cluster of billionaires operate.

50-50

The Bayesian probability of each outcome out of two alternatives will always be 50-50 a priori - without any additional information. David knew that Goliath was much stronger than him and the probability of Goliath winning was higher than 50-50. But how much higher? If the chances were 3 to 1 which chance will come first as they had only one try? At the moment when David had to make his decision he could see that the probability of him winning against Goliath was 25-75 or less because he looked at it through two 50-50 layers. It would become zero if he would opt not to fight and again apriori 50-50 if he would opt to fight.

The probability of winning is alway lower before you take the decision to fight or not to fight. If we see ahead a process consisting of dozens or hundreds of choice layers the probability of reaching the end of it seems from this distance close to zero. If you start to unfold the layers one by one you will be better informed at each step taken about the choices you have and the probability of the desired outcome will be always apriori 50-50. It may fall much lower based on the information that you obtain on the road but you will still be much better informed for making you next decision.

According to Sergey Orlovskiy, the founder of one of the leading computer games producing companies Nival Interactive, the 50-50 ratio is the most attractive risk/reward ratio for a computer games' player. Once again we come across the main principle of the investment of time - to make enjoyable as many sensations which are under our control as we can.

How many startups, do you think survive in the United States after five years? Cognitive bias suggests us the proportion in the ballpark of 10-20%. What is the actual figure given by the Small Business Administration of the Bureau of Labour Statistics? You, probably, already guessed right. It's 50%.

Many people were taken by surprise by the Brexit vote and the victory of Donald Trump. Some people even call these events Black Swans. However in the both cases the probabilities of either outcome were clearly split almost evenly as all polls showed to us. Members of the cluster of billionaires by recognizing the obvious don't try to influence the outcome as much as they try to get ready to either outcome.

Stopping Time

The definition of a stopping time in Wikipedia is so complicated that I prefer not to define it at all in the terms of probability theory. If before going to a casino I decide that I will play until I lose $ 600 or till 5 AM then I have a stopping rule and two alternatives of a stopping time: whichever of them comes earlier that will become the actual stopping time. If I decide that I will play until I beat my previous winning record it will not be a stopping rule and I will not have a stopping time because the decision on stopping requires information about the future as well as the present and past.

Why the concept of a stopping time is important for the members of the cluster? You should have no stopping time for following your passion, calling or purpose, whichever name you prefer. However for each step on your way, for each iteration you need a stopping time and a stopping rule. Especially it's true for unpredictable conditions, because stopping rule enables you to act at a stopping time without the need to foresee the future or to know past and present.

I was wondering all the time how the members of the cluster of billionaires mange to undertake and bring to successful completion so many projects simultaneously. Elon Musk says that he never thought he would run Space-X and Tesla Motors simultaneously. He just ended up doing so because he failed to find an adequate CEO for Tesla. He tried, probably, several times. He failed. There was a stopping time. He had to look for another option upon reaching it.

You may think it's easy but a stopping time is as counterintuitive as the Monty Hall problem. Sometimes it looks like tomorrow you will finally reach the target. Yet it is stopping time and you just have to stop. A stopping time is, probably, the best single instrument of hedging risks in the environment of unpredictability. The members of the cluster of billionaires are best at using it, because their brains are not only tuned but also hardwired to do so.

Where Nurture Meets Nature

"In every animal which has not passed the limit of its development, a more frequent and continuous use of any organ gradually strengthens, develops and enlarges that organ, and gives it a power proportional to the length of time it has been so used; while the permanent disuse of any organ imperceptibly weakens and deteriorates it, and progressively diminishes its functional capacity, until it finally disappears." Jean-Baptiste Lamarck

Jean Baptiste Pierre Antoine de Monet, Chevalier de Lamarck was born on August 1, 1744, in the village of Bazentin-le-Petit in the north of France. He was the youngest of eleven children in a family with a centuries-old tradition of military service; his father and several of his brothers were soldiers. The young Lamarck entered the Jesuit seminary at Amiens around 1756, but not long after his father's death, Lamarck rode off to join the French army campaigning in Germany in the summer of 1761. In his first battle, he distinguished himself for bravery under fire and was promoted to officer. After peace was declared in 1763, Lamarck spent five years on garrison duty in the south of France, until an accidental injury forced him to leave the army...

So began the life of the scientist who was the first to propose that surrounding conditions can modify characteristics acquired during a person's lifetime, and those characteristics can be passed on to the offspring.

According to Lamarck's theory a person's make-up can change within a generation depending on environmental factors. Until now this postulate forms the basis of the underlying principles of epigenetics and provides a conceptual framework for the question of how the environment impacts an organism and its offspring.

Epigenetics is broadly defined as the ensemble of processes that link a person's genotype, or the genetic information, to its phenotype, the physical and biological expression of this genetic information. These processes regulate gene activity. They can activate or inactivate genes, alter the amount of protein synthesized or expressed by a gene, and determine when a gene is expressed throughout the course of a lifetime. By implementing such changes, epigenetic processes regulate gene activity in a dynamic way.

Recent work in the field of neurobiology has revealed that epigenetic processes are essential for complex brain functions. These findings suggest that memory performance can easily be modulated, whether impaired or improved, by epigenetic processes.

Epigenetic processes are also fundamental for cellular development. During the successive phases of prenatal and postnatal development, rapid changes occur in the organization of the nervous system and the body.

Experiences during adulthood can also dynamically and persistently modify the epigenome. One of the most striking examples occurs in identical (monozygotic) twins, who have the same genome but often vary greatly in their susceptibility to disease.

Unlike the DNA sequence, epigenetic processes are dynamic and not fixed, although some can persist for long periods of time, up to several years or a lifetime. Further, they are strongly influenced by the environment and by exposure to external factors. Both positive and negative factors can modulate the epigenome.

X-Men

"The X-Men is a fictional team of superheroes appearing in American comic books published by Marvel Comics. Created by writer Stan Lee and artist/co-writer Jack Kirby, the characters first appeared in The X-Men #1 (September 1963). They are among the most recognizable and successful intellectual properties of Marvel Comics, appearing in numerous books, television shows, films, and video games.

The X-Men are mutants, a subspecies of humans who are born with superhuman abilities. The X-Men fight for peace and equality between normal humans and mutants in a world where antimutant bigotry is fierce and widespread."

Source: Wikipedia

"Feared and hated by humans because they're different, the X-Men are heroic mutants, individuals born with special powers who've sworn to use their gifts to protect mutants as well as humans."

Source: Marvel.com

"Mutants: born with extraordinary abilities, and yet still, they are children stumbling in the dark, searching for guidance. A gift can often be a curse. Give someone wings, and they may fly too close to the sun. Give them the power of prophecy, and they may live in fear of the future. Give them the greatest gift of all, powers beyond imagination, and they may think they are meant to rule the world." Professor X says in the movie X-Men: Apocalypse.

The above words may as well refer to the way how the rest of the world is treating the members of the cluster of billionaires. If the article in Wikipedia mentions that x-men are subspecies of humans and draws the line between mutants and normal humans the narrative of Marvel, the creator and owner of the x-men franchise, is crystal clear: x-men are mutants and therefore they are not human.

The same attitude towards the members of the cluster of billionaires is widespread among the members of the cluster of consumers which genuinely believe that only them are the only normal humans.

Members of the cluster of billionaires in the beginning don't realize that their behaviour starts to differ quite visibly from the behaviour of the consumers and began to irritate the later. Members of the cluster don't break rules. They don't see them in the first place. They don't understand how one norm can be universal for for all humans. With their scientific approach to life they don't realise that there can be rules which protect people from making mistakes. With their probabilistic approach to life they don't realize that someone spends a lot of time and resources on trying to regulate something that can not be regulated in the first place. They see opportunities where other people see only problems; and they can't understand why other people can not make improvement so obvious seen from cluster members' point of view.

As they grew older and, especially if they make billions and become celebrities they learn to mimic the behavior of 'normal' people. Often the learning comes hard way.

***

Fawzi Kamel, a longtime driver in Uber's original, high-end Uber Black service, was unhappy on that Sunday night in early February 2017 as he was unhappy almost every night since he had to file for bankruptcy last year. In his view drivers like him were the real investors of Uber but they had to struggle with lower fares and Uber's cheaper services undercutting their business. At the same time sone angel investors who once put only $ 20 000 into Uber now made millions.

It is not known what he thought when he discovered Uber's CEO Travis Kalanick jammed in the middle of the back seat of Fawzi's car between two female friends. Kalanick shimmied to Maroon 5's Don't Wanna Know clutching his smartphone. Fawzi didn't become happier for sure when Kalanick answering one of his companions question about Uber having a hard year said: "That's kind of how I roll. I make sure every year is a hard year. If it's easy I'm not pushing hard enough."

Fawzi's unhappiness, probably, reached the tipping point when the ride ended and Kalanick's companions hopped out of the car although the conversation started on a seemingly friendly note.

Karmel:"You have a good one."

Kalanick: "Good to see you man."

Kamel: "Good to see you, too."

Kalanick thought the conversation was over. Kamel didn't think so. In a while he was prepared to say everything.

Kamel: "You're raising the standards, and you're dropping the prices."

Kalanick: "We're not dropping the prices on black."

Kamel: "But in general the whole price is—"

Kalanick: "We have to; we have competitors; otherwise, we'd go out of business."

Kamel: "Competitors? Man, you had the business model in your hands. You could have the prices you want, but you choose to buy everybody a ride."

Kalanick: "No, no no. You misunderstand me. We started high-end. We didn't go low-end because we wanted to. We went low-end because we had to because we'd be out of business."

Kamel: "What? Lyft? It's a piece of cake right there."

Kalanick: "It seems like a piece of cake because I've beaten them. But if I didn't do the things I did, we would have been beaten, I promise."

...

Kamel: "But people are not trusting you anymore. ... I lost $97,000 because of you. I'm bankrupt because of you. Yes, yes, yes. You keep changing every day. You keep changing every day."

Kalanick: "Hold on a second, what have I changed about Black? What have I changed?"

Kamel: "You changed the whole business. You dropped the prices."

Kalanick: "On black?"

Kamel: "Yes, you did."

Kalanick begins to lose his temper. "Bullshit," he says.

Kamel: "We started with $20."

Kalanick: "Bullshit."

Kamel: "We started with $20. How much is the mile now, $2.75?"

Kalanick: "You know what?"

Kamel: "What?"

Kalanick: "Some people don't like to take responsibility for their own shit. They blame everything in their life on somebody else. Good luck!"

The entire episode reminded me a funny scene from Liar Liar movie with Jim Carrey. It turned out not so funny for Kalanick however when Fawzi Kamel handed dashcam footage of the incident to Bloomberg.

"Like Facebook's Mark Zuckerberg before him, Kalanick is trying to learn how to empathize and communicate. But Kalanick at 40, compared with 32-year-old Zuckerberg, is having to change his ways later in life, and he's often reluctant to tread too far from his intuitions. Even when Kalanick tries to express empathy in his own way—which often means jumping into a dialectical argument of sorts— his temper can occasionally flare." Eric Newcomer wrote in Bloomberg Technology and it was the most modest criticism of Kalanick in the media. The video, according to Nicole Gallucci from Mashable, showed Kalanick "being an asshole to his own Uber driver."

Kalanick sent the following note to all Uber employees on the same day when the dashboard video surfaced:

"By now I'm sure you've seen the video where I treated an Uber driver disrespectfully. To say that I am ashamed is an extreme understatement. My job as your leader is to lead...and that starts with behaving in a way that makes us all proud. That is not what I did, and it cannot be explained away.

It's clear this video is a reflection of me—and the criticism we've received is a stark reminder that I must fundamentally change as a leader and grow up. This is the first time I've been willing to admit that I need leadership help and I intend to get it.

I want to profoundly apologize to Fawzi, as well as the driver and rider community, and to the Uber team.

Travis"

Members of the cluster of billionaires differ from the members of the cluster of consumers in some respects which I am trying to outline in this book and which, probably, account for much less than one percent of everything that makes us human. In all the other respects they are just human. However, one of their specific features makes their direct interaction with the cluster of consumers difficult. Consumers believe that billionaires are the superheroes from Marvel comics and movies and expect them to behave like ones. Members of the cluster of billionaires feel like just ordinary people. They don't change when they acquire billions. They keep treating all people around like equals. For consumers it often means that they are rude and lack empathy.

Babes & Balls

On the first Weekend of March 2017 Dropbox CEO and founder Drew Houston celebrated his birthday with a dinner at Babu Ji in the Mission District in San Francisco,. Facebook CEO Mark Zuckerberg and Uber CEO Travis Kalanick attended.

After the dinner, the three CEOs went to play some ping pong at SPiN in San Francisco where "Babes & Balls: Breakfast at Tiffany's" party took place.

When photos surfaced within the "Babes & Balls" Facebook photo album of them playing ping pong a headline shit-storm happened:

- Uber CEO Travis Kalanick played ping pong with Mark Zuckerberg at a party called 'Babes and Balls'

- Mark Zuckerberg and Travis Kalanick laugh it up at 'Babes and Balls' party

- 'Sexist' Tech Moguls Under Fire For Attending Exclusive 'Babes and Balls' Party

"It makes sense, while under so much pressure, that Kalanick would want to kick back and enjoy a fun night with his friends. He's also known to play by his own rules and apologize later, if at all. But you'd hope that the men who are shaping our culture, and setting examples for thousands of young founders every day, would recognize the public perception of being at a party called Babes & Balls. That they have a responsibility to represent massive workforces, an industry and entrepreneurs everywhere." Wrote Techcrunch's Jordan Crook referring to the story from the above chapter and a scandal about Uber treating badly female developers hence the word 'sexist' in a headline above.

The accusations came from Susan Fowler Rigetti, a 25-year old site reliability engineer, who had worked at the company for a little over a year. She wrote an entry on her personal blog called simply: "Reflecting on one very, very strange year at Uber."

Uber reacted by bringing in former Attorney General Eric Holder to lead an independent investigation into the claims, assigning Arianna Huffington who joined the company's board in 2016 to improve the company's culture, holding an hour-long session with HR to answer questions after the weekly company meeting. Travis Kalanick met with more than 100 women working for the company to hear their concerns over sexism.

Rigetti posted on Twitter that people were being contacted for "personal and intimate info" about her, causing another shit-storm as many concluded that Uber was behind these actions.

Uber sweared it's not them but Rigetti retained a law firm just in case. The scandal was over just a few days before the Babes and Balls party.

The Mutation

I started Cluster of Billionaires as a book about self made billionaires whom I knew personally or whose many hours long interviews I watched on the web with the old headhunter's scrutiny. I've spotted some common features in them and decided to season them with a gravy from neuroscience, psychology and biology to add more taste and flavour.

Every book, however, starts to dictate its own terms after you write maybe 50 pages or little more. First, a comparison between human and ant behavior grew from a metaphor into an important line of thought. Then, Bayesian probability and Markov process popped up out of nowhere.

The tipping point took place at the third day after I began to record interesting thoughts about the book on video for a crowdfunding campaign. When I spoke about epigenetic transformation in ants it suddenly struck me that changes which I observed in billionaires may also be epigenetic by origin.

Epigenetic changes take place with many species in nature when some genes already present in their DNA get turned on or off by either social or environmental factors, or a combination of both. In the case of ants such changes are very deep internally — they totally change their physiology — but have no visible signs at the outside. They are achieved by ants taking part in ritualized fightings in which they fight long and hard but without hurting their opponents. As a result they make their dopamine level to rise 3–4 fold with that effect lasting for hours. So they achieve powerful and long lasting enough effect to trigger and complete an epigenetic mutation.

Let's have a closer look at self made billionaires. With all their passion for what they are doing, their calling for action, readiness to take risks, resilience to failures and more they expose themselves to factors which already have a rather strong effect each separately but produce a totally overwhelming impact if they are combined and last for years. Can we imagine that some deep and sustainable epigenetic mutations may take place altering the physiology of their brains? My answer is: "Yes."

The process of transformation should start long before they actually become billionaires. If we know what we are looking for, we may become able to spot future billionaires and, maybe, even nurture them. Scientists promise that soon it will become possible to trace epigenetic regulation of genes with a simple blood test.

The idea that seemed then totally nuts came to my mind less than a week ago. Now I know that epigenetics is a hot topic in neuroscience because the human brain undergoes more epigenetic transformations than any other organ of any species. Epigenetic changes affect our memory and control the development of our cognitive abilities. They are deep, sometimes even heritable but reversible .

Recent research proves that "changes in neuronal activity result in robust changes in expression and activity of multiple DNA methylation-associated proteins with an essential role for neuronal health and function." Translated into simple English it means that the activity of our brain itself trigger significant epigenetic changes in the brain.

"Over the course of only a few years, we have witnessed a proliferation of epigenetic studies in the human brain, ranging from exploration of chromatin structures at a specific genomic locus to genome-wide epigenome mapping in defined cell types, generally with signal-to-noise ratios and signal quality comparable to those obtained in animal brains. Work from multiple groups, focusing mainly on human association cortex, points to large-scale remodeling of DNA and histone methylation landscapes during the late prenatal phase and early postnatal phase and early childhood, with comparatively less dramatic changes during subsequent stages of development and aging. Still, hundreds of promoters are subject to epigenetic changes that seemingly continue into old age, and these data, taken together, leave little doubt that chromatin structures undergo remodeling throughout the lifespan of the human brain, including neurons and other terminally differentiated cells." Researchers conclude stating that epigenetic remodelling of the human brain continues throughout its entire lifespan and envisaging that the future development in this field "will provide a powerful tool to gain deep and unprecedented insights into the genomic foundations of cognition and emotion."

Now you can see why I am trying to explore in this book the factors which may trigger and support the 'billionaire mutation' and to observe the implications of such a mutation as well.

The word 'mutation' is a bit provocative, of course, especially given the fact that epigenetic change is reversible because genes can be switched on and off, but I use it to emphasise the power and depth of this invisible but radical transformation.

The most recent findings suggest that it will be possible to trace epigenetic changes in our brain by simple saliva tests. "Additional convergence has been reported between methylation patterns in blood and saliva, with some comparisons further suggesting that patterns in DNA derived from saliva rather than blood better map onto variability in brain function." It may sound like a pure science fiction but soon we might need only to spit to find out if we are on track to the cluster of billionaires.

Winning enhances our brain, power damages it. Regular winning by beating their own records in a really hard race when only their passion makes them keep going may eventually turn members of the cluster of billionaires into the human analog of tetrahedrons which due to their state and shape can form quasicrystals from entropy itself. Members of the cluster may become solid enough, get the right shape and be pulled together in their cluster closely enough to each other to take part in one of the most magnificent transformations which exist in nature - the emergence of order out of chaos. It's a pure speculation though but it is so interesting that I couldn't resist putting it into this book.

Tetrahedra

Tetrahedra is a plural of tetrahedron. Tetrahedron is a solid figure with four triangular faces. If you want to make its definition more detailed you can add that it has six straight edges, and four vertex corners. Then you will not be able to add anything else to this description. It's solid and it has a clearly defined shape.

Members of the cluster of billionaires sometimes remind me tetrahedra. They are also solid and their shape is clearly defined. Their angles are sharp like the angles of tetrahedrons.

Computational physicist Sharon Glotzer uses tetrahedra to create order out of chaos. Her approach is completely counterintuitive. "We typically think entropy means disorder, and so a disordered structure would have more entropy than an ordered structure." She said in an interview to Quanta magazine. "That can be true under certain circumstances, but it's not always true, and in these cases, it's not. I prefer to think of entropy as related to options: The more options a system of particles has to arrange itself, the higher the entropy. In certain circumstances, it's possible for a system to have more options — more possible arrangements — of its building blocks if the system is ordered."

In Sharon's computer simulations each tetrahedron tries to maximize the space in which it can jiggle in different directions following the increase of entropy. As a result she gets the most complicated entropically stabilized structure that anyone has ever seen. Tetrahedrons get arranged with one another based solely on entropy, meaning they have no direct interactions between them — they don't want to stick together; there's no charges; there's no chemical bonds; there's nothing but entropy that clinking them together into complex quasicrystal structures.

Sharon calls this process emergence and seeks the rules that govern emergence in general from quasicrystals to living organisms. She herself suggests a parallel between the emergence of quasi crystallized structures from entropy to processes which sometimes take place in groups of people. "That's emergence! It is emergence! When the group gets big enough all of a sudden, and you have the right mix of people, it's amazing some of the directions that are coming out that I never would have anticipated before."

"Stay solid and keep your shape." Another principle of the cluster of billionaires says.

Maximization of the number of options in which direction to move looks to my mind exactly like the maximization of the freedom of choice. I can easily imagine members of the cluster of billionaires in places of tetrahedrons constantly seeking for as many options as possible and creating quasi crystallized structure with other people like them having in it the same maximum number of options without any risk of collisions between them though. Looks like a model for the ideal society for me - the cluster of billionaires. Question remain: how the cluster of consumers will be organized and how the interaction between the clusters will take place.

Where now?

I first saw the term 'emergence' in a book of Ilya Prigogine, a Belgian physical chemist and Nobel Laureate noted for his work on dissipative structures, complex systems, and irreversibility. The book's name in English was 'Order out of Chaos'.

"At present humanity is going through a bifurcation process due to information technology. We can of course quote other social bifurcations related to fossil energy: coal, oil which lead to the industrial society. Now we have the information technology which leads to the networked society. What will be the effect of the present bifurcation? Because of the scales involved we can expect a larger role of non linear terms therefore larger fluctuations and increased instability.

Will the networked society lead to some form of unification of humanity? This is not certain. My friend Professor Jean-Louis Deneubourg made the remark that networked societies exist involving social insects. We know today about 12,000 ant species. Their colony sizes are ranging from a few individuals to 20 millions of individuals. It is remarkable that the behavior of the small ant society and of the large ant societies are quite different. In a small insect society, individuals know at any moment what they must do. They go foraging, they come back to share their prey, they behave independently. However, once the society becomes large, coordination becomes the major problem. There appear complex collective structures that spontaneously emerge from simple autocatalytic interactions between numerous individuals and with the environment mediated by chemical communication. In small insect societies, the complexity is localized at the individual. In large ant societies, complexity is more on the level on the interactions between the individuals. It is certainly not a coincidence that in the largest and most integrated societies, that is in the army ants and termites, the individuals are practically blind.

The evolution from the small ant society to large ant society was the result of qualitative changes involving discontinuities. Such type of discontinuities appear in many fields of physics, chemistry and biology. They are associated with bifurcations. Bifurcations play an important role in our present view of nature. They lead to multiple possibilities which are associated to probabilities. They destroy the classical deterministic view of nature."

Prigogine wrote in his message to the president of the Club of Rome Bertrandt Schneider in 1999.

The name "bifurcation" was first introduced in 1885 by Henri Poincaré, a French mathematician, theoretical physicist, engineer, and philosopher of science. A bifurcation occurs when a small smooth change made to the parameter values of a system causes a sudden qualitative change in its behaviour. That's a scientific definition. In the common language bifurcation means just splitting of something into two. We can agree or disagree with Prigogine but for me 18 years which passed since he wrote the above text prove that he was right.

"When we look at social media we see it as a continuum and a continuum is from accumulation to instant expression. If you trip the memory line seven-ten years ago you take a bunch of photos with your camera to party and you ran home and maybe the next day you plug in your camera and you upload your photos to the internet and friends can look on them. That's really the accumulation model. Right? The fascinating side about our business is that mobile phones have unlocked the ability to instantly express yourself." Evan Spiegel explains the value proposition of Snapchat, the image messaging app that he launched out of his living room in father's house in 2011 and brought public in 2017 at $ 24 billion valuation. I wonder if you see the resemblance between the transformation of ant colonies described by Prigogine and the movement from accumulation to instant expression on a continuum presented by Spiegel. I definitely see it especially given that cameras more and more replace keyboards and likes and shares work more and more like pheromones from the communication between ants.

The system of human civilization has entered a phase of instability. Its fluctuations intensify. Ilya Prigozhin, wrote that the world around us became dangerous, full of surprises and changes when we let uncertainty into it. Unpredictability and instability frighten. But it is under these conditions that negligible forces can initiate changes, which will radically reorganize the entire system. Order will emerge out of chaos at a new, higher, energy level. This can occur due to the autocatalytic process. Consolidation of the cluster of billionaires is an autocatalytic process, each participant of which, not only facilitates the transformation, but also participates in it.

Anternet

Deborah M. Gordon at Stanford has been following a population of 300 harvester ant colonies for more than 25 years. She discovered that many perceptions of the public and even scientists about ant behavior are entirely wrong. The longest standing misunderstanding is the projection of dominance models to the ant behaviour. It starts with naming 'queen' an adult reproducing female ant in an ant colony. Ants' queen doesn't control anything except reproduction.

It seems that human willingness to introduce some sort of dominance into ant colonies emerges from our inability to accept the fact that ants can demonstrate so highly coordinated and organized behavior without any coordinators or managers at all. The intelligent behavior of ant colonies achieved without any coordination or management appears absolutely counterintuitive to humans which only know societies based on some sort of dominance hierarchy. Ants, however, live on Earth some 120-130 million years longer than humans. Therefore, their networked communities may well show in which direction the evolution of humanity is going.

Interestingly, there are close parallels between social networks of ants and human-engineered networks. The group of researcher led by Deborah found that the algorithm desert ants use to regulate foraging is very similar to the Traffic Control Protocol (TCP) used to regulate data traffic on the internet. Both ant and human networks use feedback loops: either from acknowledgements that trigger the transmission of the next data packet, or from food-laden returning foragers that trigger the exit of another outgoing forager.

A feedback loop allows TCP to run congestion avoidance: If acks (acknowledgement signals) return at a slower rate than the data was sent out, that indicates that there is little bandwidth available, and the source throttles data transmission down accordingly. If acks return quickly, the source boosts its transmission speed. The process determines how much bandwidth is available and throttles data transmission accordingly.

A forager ant won't return to the nest until it finds food. If seeds are plentiful, foragers return faster, and more ants leave the nest to forage. If, however, ants begin returning empty handed, the search is slowed, and perhaps called off.

Ants spend water to get water. Their organisms lose water when they are foraging and they replenish their water balance by eating some seeds collected during foraging. Their system of negative feedback stops foraging effort when water loses raise higher than gains. Similarly in the internet, the TCP protocol also prevents the system from sending data out when there's no bandwidth available.

Researchers also found that ants followed two other protocols of TCP. One is known as slow start, which describes how a source sends out a large wave of packets at the beginning of a transmission to gauge bandwidth; similarly, when the harvester ants begin foraging, they send out foragers to scope out food availability before scaling up or down the rate of outgoing foragers.

Another protocol, called time-out, occurs when a data transfer link breaks or is disrupted, and the source stops sending packets. Similarly, when foragers are prevented from returning to the nest for more than 20 minutes, no more foragers leave the nest.

From the behavior of ants we can learn some counterintuitive solutions for the organisation of our communications and commute.

For instance, ants speed up instead of slowing down in response to a higher density of traffic on their trails. When the researchers at the University of Halle-Wittenberg in Germany increased the supply of food by leaving food next to the trail, ants accelerated their speed by 50 percent. This was despite more than double the density of traffic.

When food increases in supply, more forager ants are sent out to carry it back to the nest. With this increase in ant density, the number of encounters between outbound and incoming individuals increases. Researchers suggest that the encounters provide an opportunity for ants to swap information and to change their behavior according to conditions.

After reading the above paragraph I suddenly imagined cars on a highway bumping into each other on high speed to exchange information. We shouldn't, of course try to directly mock the behaviour of ants but there are striking similarities between the ant colony behaviour and the behaviour of the evolving human networked society.

Simple Complexity

"Jack Ma has built e-commerce firm Alibaba into a behemoth. Its IPO in New York in 2014 set a record as the world's biggest public stock offering. Though dogged by criticism that Alibaba doesn't do enough to limit the sale of fakes, Ma is leading Alibaba to ever higher sales. A record $463 billion of business transactions were conducted on Alibaba's retail platforms in the fiscal year through March 2016. The company set a goal of creating 10 million profitable businesses and 100 million jobs in the next 20 years. Ma made headlines at the World Economic Forum in Davos, Switzerland in January, when he told CNBC that America has no one to blame but itself for its economic issues. Beyond e-commerce, in October 2016 Alibaba's film unit forged an alliance with Steven Spielberg's Amblin Partners, giving a potential boost to a struggling effort so far in the entertainment industry." Forbes, 2017

"The tools that serve large colonies well, therefore, are redundancy and minimal information. Enormous ant colonies function using very simple interactions..." Deborah M. Gordon explains. "A colony is analogous to a brain where there are lots of neurons, each of which can only do something very simple, but together the whole brain can think."

The cluster of billionaires does not accept complexity in interpersonal interaction. Understanding comes quickly. All actions are binary. As in the case when complexity in molecular architecture allows for simplification of reaction schemes, the complexity of the architecture of members of the cluster determines the simplicity of interaction between them.

"Simple". Jack Ma, founder and CEO of the internet commerce giant Alibaba likes to repeat, talking about the secrets of his success.

"That's been one of my mantras -- focus and simplicity. Simple can be harder than complex: You have to work hard to get your thinking clean to make it simple. But it's worth it in the end because once you get there, you can move mountains." Steve Jobs said in his interview with Andy Reinhardt for Business Week in May 1998.

The protocol for understanding of meanings, in the words of Uri Hasson, in the brain of representatives of the cluster of billionaires is so complex, and their immersion into the joint context is so deep that it allows them to catch the meaning literally from a half-word. But this is within their cluster. People from the cluster of consumers, even if they are experts in the subject under discussion, can not make sense out of what a person from the cluster of billionaires says. They lack the right context. And vice versa.

Coupled Brains

When people talk to each other, being in the same context, the fMRI images of activation of their brains gradually becomes identical. A coupling of their brains provides almost complete transfer of meaning. People begin to work as nodes of a synchronized cluster. This phenomenon is described by Uri Hasson. In practice, many of us experienced it ourselves at rare moments of wonderfully smooth work or play. There is even a term for this: "flow". Members of the cluster of billionaires are able to work in the state of flow for years.

"When it comes to getting started, good-to-great leaders understand three simple truths. First, if you begin with "who," you can more easily adapt to a fast-changing world. If people get on your bus because of where they think it's going, you'll be in trouble when you get 10 miles down the road and discover that you need to change direction because the world has changed. But if people board the bus principally because of all the other great people on the bus, you'll be much faster and smarter in responding to changing conditions. Second, if you have the right people on your bus, you don't need to worry about motivating them. The right people are self-motivated: Nothing beats being part of a team that is expected to produce great results. And third, if you have the wrong people on the bus, nothing else matters. You may be headed in the right direction, but you still won't achieve greatness. Great vision with mediocre people still produces mediocre results. " Jim Collins wrote in his great book "From Good to Great."

As Peter Thiel did he also came to the conclusion that selection of right people is the key factor of creating a great company. It was difficult for him to understand which people are right as it was to me, when I interviewed dozens of top managers looking for outstanding leadership competencies. These super-heroes did not do anything unusual. They were not great, but they built great companies. They were just from the cluster of billionaires.

"The structure of the shared external environment shapes our neural responses and behavior. Some aspects of the environment are determined by the physical environment. Other aspects, however, are determined by a community of individuals, who together establish a shared set of rules (behaviors) that shape and constrain the perception and actions of each member of the group." Researchers from Uri Hasson's group conclude. "Coupled brains can create new phenomena, including verbal and nonverbal communication systems and interpersonal social institutions that could not have emerged in species that lack brain-to-brain coupling. Thus, just as the Copernican revolution simplified rather than complicated our understanding of the physical world, embracing brain-to-brain coupling as a reference system may simplify our understanding of behavior by illuminating new forces that operate among individuals and shape our social world."

To Alpha Centauri

In my investigation I was going to prove by the example of self made billionaires that universal human values make a person successful. It didn't work. I wanted to believe that they were some very ethical people, but all that I learned about them completely contradicted this hope. No, they were not monsters, bloodsuckers, money-grubbers, as communist propaganda liked to portray them. They were just like ordinary people. With all the inherent flaws. They, like everyone else, got spoiled with power and money.

I took a closer look at philanthropy and noticed some differences in values. Billionaires are kinder than ordinary people contrary to some recent research papers which are trying to prove that people become less empathic as they get richier. Maybe, these findings of researchers are relevant to relatively rich members of the consumer cluster but actions speak for the members of the cluster of billionaires much more evidently that some very limited experiments in which researcher manipulated participant's economic status feelings. Billionaires recently began to commit philanthropic acts which totally shock representatives of the cluster of consumers.

For example, Yuri Milner, instead of buying a kilometer long boat, financed a search for extraterrestrial civilizations; and then - a flight to Alpha Centauri.

In December 2016 a constellation of tech billionaires, A-list celebrities, and preeminent scientists convened at NASA's Ames Research Center in Silicon Valley for an Oscars-style ceremony of Breakthrough Prize. The Prize was established when Yuri Milner and his wife Julia said they would annually reward theoretical physicists for outstanding scientific achievements, starting in 2012. Since then, the number of disciplines has expanded as more patrons have joined the cause, such as Facebook's Mark Zuckerberg and his wife Priscilla Chan, Google's Sergey Brin and his ex wife - founder of biotech firm 23andMe's Anne Wojcicki, and Alibaba's Jack Ma and his wife Cathy Zhang.

I worked with Milner in the early 2000s, when he only began investing in the Internet, and I did not notice anything extravagant about him. Although, yes, already then he behaved as a representative of the cluster of billionaires. I remember that he corrected by hand the numbers of fees in my proposal and returned it to me with his signature. Honestly, I, who was used to long discussions about fees and terms, was slightly taken aback. I called Milner, to bargain and ... confirmed that I was starting to work. The numbers inscribed by him suited me.

The number and scale of philanthropy initiatives are growing with a stunning speed. I mention here just a few of them.

To March 1, 2017, the Giving Pledge, launched in 2010 by Bill Gates and Warren Buffett, had 157 "pledgers" (a family or couple counts as one) in 17 countries. It was originally limited to the United States but went international in 2013.

In September 2016 Warren Buffett told Yahoo Finance editor Andy Serwer via video conference that he is most proud of the younger signatories, like the co-founders of Airbnb. "I tell them, every one of them is worth 10 of me because you're going to have young people, particularly in this day and age, get wealthy very early and they're going to look to the people who are their heroes, whether it's Mark Zuckerberg or Brian Chesky," he said.

In April 2016 billionaire tech entrepreneur Sean Parker (Napster, Facebook) announced that he is giving $250 million through his foundation to launch the Parker Institute for Cancer Immunotherapy, a collaboration between some of the US top cancer research institutes that aims to accelerate the development of breakthrough immunotherapies.

In September 2016 Facebook co-founder Mark Zuckerberg and his wife, Priscilla Chan, on Wednesday announced a $3 billion effort to accelerate scientific research with the goal of "curing all disease in our children's lifetime."

John Paul DeJoria, who according to Forbes estimates is worth $3.2 billion, signed the Giving Pledge in 2011, committing to give away more than half of his total net worth. While his JP's Peace, Love and Happiness Foundation has already been giving away millions, he's also building new social businesses like Rok Mobile, which doesn't have its own phones but sells mobile plans via SIM cards.

In March 2017 Bill and Melinda Gates—who are also custodians of legendary investor Warren Buffet's billions— have joined forces with Pierre Omidyar, founder of eBay, to fund the 'Radiant Earth' project, a repository and archive of the world's satellite, aerial and drone imagery.

As The Guardian reports, there are those who see serious risks in the era of super-giving that started with the Gates Foundation, and who worry that our warm fuzzy feelings are blinding us to the broader implications. "What's curious is that even benign, obvious criticisms are seen as violating the sacrosanct sphere of private giving," says Linsey McGoey, senior lecturer in sociology at the University of Essex and author of a book about "philanthrocapitalism" called No Such Thing as a Free Gift. "There's this idea that there should be no constraints. But the problem is that such gifts exert sway over decision-making that affects the lives of millions. So it needs to be monitored."

When some of the workers in one ant colony began to transform into gamergates, researchers removed them from the colony. They found that these winner ants had already begun to produce elevated levels of dopamine – more than other workers, but still less than full-fledged gamergates.

Researchers then placed these transforming winner workers into another colony. The regular workers there recognized the changes in the winner workers and exhibited "policing" behavior, holding down the transforming ants so that they couldn't move. Within 24 hours, the dopamine levels in the transforming workers had dropped back to normal; they were just regular worker ants again.

And beyond..

The cluster of billionaires, in the process of further consolidation, can grow into a collective mind of a new type - with a level of awareness and speed that has never been seen before. It will be a fundamentally different intellect in relation to the artificial. Where an artificial superintelligence will calculate, the human superintelligence will throw dice. And they will agree up to something, it seems to me.

At the 2017 World Government Summit in Dubai Elon Musk said: "The way to escape human obsolescence, in the end, may be by having some sort of merger of biological intelligence and machine intelligence. We're already cyborgs. Your phone and your computer are extensions of you, but the interface is through finger movements or speech, which are very slow. For a meaningful partial-brain interface, I think we're roughly four or five years away."

What about us, simple mortals from the cluster of consumers? Why do we need them? Why do they need us?

Roughly we can imagine that all humans have a switch in their heads that change between the upper and the lower gear. Brains at the upper gear are thinking much faster but they need to be synchronised with the slower brains. Switching the gear back and forth for each communication is a huge loss of energy. Clusterization may help to resolve this problem by making faster brains and slower brains interacting directly only with the brains of the same speed. Communication between the cluster may happen through a computer algorithm that will automatically adjust the speed.

When scientists look at colonies of ants which we already have used in this book as a model of networked society they notice that the vast majority of ants is doing nothing all the time. Furthermore as the colony grows larger the share of working ants becomes smaller. If in a group of 30 ants 60% of ants were doing nothing then in a group of 300 ants already 80% of critters were working hard on not doing anything at all. As scientists yet don't know the reason why the proportion of lazy ants is growing together with the size of the colony they speculate that this practice helps the colony to optimise its energy consumption. Not working ants may also serve as a buffer to be activated in emergency situations or in case of a major expansion.

It seems quite obvious that the members of the cluster of billionaires at the level of 2-20% of the entire Earth's population depending of the size of humanity together with robots will be capable of easily satisfying all the needs of the cluster of consumers. They will also produce enough resources to pursue their most ambitious goals. However, scaling up of humanity and expansion to outer space may require a significant increase in the size of the cluster of billionaires. By that time people will, most probably, already abandon the name 'billionaires' and will call them something like 'self made minds.'

It is premature to say if the epigenetic mutation of billionaire really takes place. In case it exists self made minds will most probably be still unable to pass this mutation to their children because switching right genes on requires some very strong environmental factors to be applied for a long period of time. On the other hand the mutation may happen to a human of any age, race or gender provided that he or she spends enough time under the influence of relevant epigenetic factors. Some of the most important such factors I tried to outline in this book: passion, action, experimentation, authenticity, or in the other words, ability to enjoy meaningful and risky life and to constantly grow as fast as it is humanly possible.

I can't guarantee you, of course, that the mutation will definitely happen if you follow this path. It will be fun but it will be extremely hard, and the hardship will make the fun much sweeter.

As you might already have guessed, the path of representatives of the cluster of billionaires, who have not yet earned billions, among the representatives of the consumer cluster is by no means covered with roses. They are not understood. The ideas they offer are rejected, decisions are ridiculed. They are reproached with stubbornness, absurd character and excessive risk. Indeed, when one of them monetizes, all of their numerous shortcomings (from the point of view of consumers) immediately turn into virtues, but in the beginning their path is thorny. But this is not their choice. They just live like this and can not do otherwise. Therefore, in relation to them a little tolerance will not hurt anyone. First of all, it won't hurt consumers who dream of becoming billionaires.

Happiness of Understanding

The fact is that understanding the context of the cluster of billionaires is available to any person, even if his brain has not yet reached the stage of radical plasticity. Furthermore, tolerance and attempts to understand can serve as a trigger for changes in the brain. To do this, you need to pair your brains through communication. Strangely enough, the easiest way is to communicate with actual billionaires. First, in this case, you know for sure that you see a real representative of the cluster of billionaires, not just a preacher, a speculator or a mad projecteur. Secondly, for the coupling of brains, communication should not necessarily be two-sided. It is enough to listen and watch their interviews, preferably with members of the same cluster with them. For example, watch at YouTube the fireside chat of the founder of Sun Microsystems Vinod Khosla with the founders of Google Sergey Brin and Larry Page. Internet is full of such conversations. You just have to be patient, because at first it may be uninteresting and incomprehensible. The more you love to talk, the harder it will be for you to listen. We must learn to invest our time, there's nothing we can do. And where is the joy? - you may ask. Joy is in understanding. There is a small nuance: if your joy from other people understanding you is a cost, the joy of your understanding other people is an investment of time. Because, when something is clear to you, you explaining this thing is practically guaranteed understood by others.

That's all. Welcome to the brave new world!

December 15, 2016 - March 31, 2017, Sosnovka

Annex #1. Featured Billionaires

Jeff Bezos https://www.forbes.com/profile/jeff-bezos/

Len Blavatnik https://www.forbes.com/profile/len-blavatnik/

Warren Buffett https://www.forbes.com/profile/warren-buffett/

Richard Branson
https://www.forbes.com/profile/richard-branson/

Yvon Chouinard
https://www.forbes.com/profile/yvon-chouinard/

Mikhail Fridman
https://www.forbes.com/profile/mikhail-fridman/

Reid Hoffman https://www.forbes.com/profile/reid-hoffman/

Steve Jobs

Travis Kalanick https://www.forbes.com/profile/travis-kalanick/

Andrey Kosogov
https://www.forbes.com/profile/andrei-kosogov/

Jack Ma https://www.forbes.com/profile/jack-ma/

Miguel McKelvey
https://www.forbes.com/profile/miguel-mckelvey/

Yuri Milner https://www.forbes.com/profile/yuri-milner/

Elon Musk https://www.forbes.com/profile/elon-musk/

Sean Parker https://www.forbes.com/profile/sean-parker/

Evan Spiegel https://www.forbes.com/profile/evan-spiegel/

Roustam Tariko
https://www.forbes.com/profile/roustam-tariko/

Peter Thiel https://www.forbes.com/profile/peter-thiel/

Mark Zuckerberg
https://www.forbes.com/profile/mark-zuckerberg/

Annex #2. Index

Virtuous Circle: Fireside Chat with Travis Kalanick and Arianna Huffington https://www.youtube.com/watch?v=8jY-t8tt4Hg

Snapchat's three-part business model with CEO Evan Spiegel (2015 Code Conference, Day 1) https://www.youtube.com/watch?v=AqPHordzhdw

An Invisible Wall

Uri Hasson, Associate Professor of Psychology and the Princeton Neuroscience Institute, Home https://pni.princeton.edu/faculty/uri-hasson

"Speaker– Coupled neural systems underlie the production and comprehension of naturalistic narrative speech" Lauren J. Silbert, Christopher J. Honey, Erez Simony, David Poeppel, and Uri Hasson http://www.hassonlab.com/brain-to-brain-communication

"Uri Hasson: This is your brain on communication" TED Talk http://www.ted.com/talks/uri_hasson_this_is_your_brain_on_communication#t-878437

A Planet of Ants

Ants, Ants Everywhere: and a lot more than you think https://natureisanythingbutsimple.wordpress.com/2014/01/21/ants/

Why Ants Rule the World http://www.livescience.com/747-ants-rule-world.html

2000 year-old termite mound found http://www.bbc.com/earth/story/20150729-2000-year-old-termite-mound-found

Why Termites BuildSuch Enormous Skyscrapers
http://www.bbc.com/earth/story/20151210-why-termites-build-such-enormous-skyscrapers

Radhika Nagpal, Fred Kavli Professor of Computer Science School of Engineering and Applied Sciences Wyss Institute for Biologically Inspired Engineering Harvard University
http://www.radhikanagpal.org

Ants Respond as a Collective "Superorganism" When They Sense a Predator
http://www.sciencealert.com/ants-respond-as-a-collective-superorganism-when-they-sense-a-predator

First Flowers Triggered Boom in Ant Diversity
http://www.livescience.com/4034-flowers-triggered-boom-ant-diversity.html

Order out of Chaos

Forbes/profile/Mikhail Fridman
https://www.forbes.com/profile/mikhail-fridman/

As Global Instability Spreads, the "Indigo" Economy Rises
http://www.realclearpolitics.com/articles/2016/04/29/indigo_era_a_tectonic_shift_is_reshaping_the_world_130434.html

Termites are lazy, when they aren't eating wood, UGA researcher says
http://www.caes.uga.edu/newswire/story.html?storyid=5154

Most worker ants are slackers
http://www.sciencemag.org/news/2015/10/most-worker-ants-are-slackers

Lazy Ants Make Colonies More Productive
https://www.seeker.com/lazy-ants-make-colonies-more-productive-2199658973.html

Struck Heads

Forbes 2017 Billionaires List: Meet The Richest People On The Planet
https://www.forbes.com/sites/kerryadolan/2017/03/20/forbes-2017-billionaires-list-meet-the-richest-people-on-the-planet/#2987edc262ff

North America is going to get a new billionaire every 6 days
http://www.businessinsider.com/credit-suisse-wealth-report-shows-rise-of-chinese-and-us-billionaires-2016-11

"Little Golden Calf" by Ilya Ilf and Yevgeny Petrov
https://www.amazon.com/Little-Golden-Calf-Ilya-Ilf/dp/1880100614

Peter Thiel - Signs to look for in a Successful Start-Up
https://www.youtube.com/watch?v=H_j3x8N8fpA&t=178s

5 Mega-Successful Entrepreneurs Who Are Introverts
https://www.entrepreneur.com/article/286611

The Oracle of Omaha Learns to Speak

Forbes/Profile/Warren Buffett
https://www.forbes.com/profile/warren-buffett/

Warren Buffett Used To Throw Up Before Public Speaking — Here's How He Mastered It http://www.businessinsider.com/how-warren-buffett-learned-public-speaking-2014-12

The Snowball: Warren Buffett and the Business of Life.
http://www.randomhouse.com/bantamdell/snowball/

From Zero to One billion in Four Years

Peter Thiel, From Zero to One
https://www.amazon.com/Zero-One-Notes-Startups-Future/dp/0804139296

The French Patient

Meet the Man Who Lives Normally With Damage to 90% of His Brain
http://www.sciencealert.com/a-man-who-lives-without-90-of-his-brain-is-challenging-our-understanding-of-consciousness

The Radical Plasticity Thesis: How the Brain Learns to be Conscious
https://www.ncbi.nlm.nih.gov/pmc/articles/PMC3110382/

Sure I'm sure: Prefrontal oscillations support metacognitive monitoring of decision-making
http://www.jneurosci.org/content/early/2016/12/12/JNEUROSCI.1612-16.2016

Is Your Brain Really Necessary?

Is Your Brain Really Necessary?
http://rifters.com/real/articles/Science_No-Brain.pdf

Revisiting hydrocephalus as a model to study brain resilience
http://rifters.com/real/articles/Oliveira-et-al-2012-RevisitingHydrocephalus.pdf

Is the brain really a small-world network?
https://www.ncbi.nlm.nih.gov/pmc/articles/PMC4853440/

Who Is Selected for Astronauts?

Forbes/Profile/Len Blavatnik
https://www.forbes.com/profile/len-blavatnik/

Fouad Said http://www.bilan.ch/said

The Lifelong Trip

Forbes/Profile/Yuri Milner
https://www.forbes.com/profile/yuri-milner/

How LSD Microdosing Became the Hot New Business Trip

http://www.rollingstone.com/culture/features/how-lsd-microdosing-became-the-hot-new-business-trip-20151120

Forbes/Profile/John Paul DeJoria
https://www.forbes.com/profile/john-paul-dejoria/

Why Billionaire John Paul DeJoria's Rok Mobile Is Pairing Life And Burial Insurance With A $49 Plan

https://www.forbes.com/sites/chloesorvino/2016/05/11/why-billionaire-john-paul-dejorias-rok-mobile-is-pairing-life-and-burial-insurance-with-a-49-plan/#5d6b90dd2014

Yuri Milner's Unparalleled Global Tech Gold-Mining Machine

https://www.forbes.com/sites/parmyolson/2015/03/25/yuri-milners-unparalleled-global-tech-gold-mining-machine/#1437ca997d9b

Anna Karenina principle
https://en.wikipedia.org/wiki/Anna_Karenina_principle

Dropoff

Forbes/Profile/Roustam Tariko
https://www.forbes.com/profile/roustam-tariko/

Peter Thiel, From Zero to One
https://www.amazon.com/Zero-One-Notes-Startups-Future/dp/0804139296

ŻUBRÓWKA MAKER'S BANKRUPTCY PLANS APPROVED
https://www.thespiritsbusiness.com/2017/01/zubrowka-makers-bankruptcy-plans-approved/

Amazon CEO, Jeff Bezos, sat down with Henry Blodget at Business Insider's Ignition 2014
https://www.youtube.com/watch?v=Xx92bUw7WX8

The Longest Dwarf

Forbes/Profile/Mikhail Fridman
https://www.forbes.com/profile/mikhail-fridman/

Forbes/Profile/Andrey Kosogov
https://www.forbes.com/profile/andrei-kosogov/

Disclaimer

The Mafia Photo

The PayPal Mafia: Who are they and where are Silicon Valley's richest group of men now?
http://www.telegraph.co.uk/technology/11106473/The-PayPal-Mafia-Who-are-they-and-where-are-Silicon-Valleys-richest-group-of-men-now.html

Forbes/Profile/Peter Thiel
https://www.forbes.com/profile/peter-thiel/

Forbes/Profile/Elon Musk
https://www.forbes.com/profile/elon-musk/

Forbes/Profile/Mark Zuckerberg
https://www.forbes.com/profile/mark-zuckerberg/

Forbes/Profile/Reid Hoffman
https://www.forbes.com/profile/reid-hoffman/

Forbes/Profile/Sean Parker
https://www.forbes.com/profile/sean-parker/

Shared Dominance

Study Argues 'Winner-Winner' Behavior May Shape Animal Hierarchies https://news.ncsu.edu/2016/04/penick-win-2016/

Looking at ants to find answers about aggression
http://www.cudenvertoday.org/looking-ant-battles-learn-violence/

Dopamine Turns Worker Ants Into Warrior Queens
https://news.ncsu.edu/2014/05/penick-gamergates-2014/

Peter Thicl, From Zero to One
https://www.amazon.com/Zero-One-Notes-Startups-Future/dp/0804139296

"Not Less We Praise in Sterner Days"

Eli Goldratt, The Choice
https://www.amazon.com/Choice-Revised-Eliyahu-M-Goldratt/dp/0884271935/ref=pd_sbs_14_img_0?_encoding=UTF8&psc=1&refRID=2KDQKDQYDA56WP9MGGV2

Episode 20 w/ Elon Musk http://foundation.bz/20/

Winston Churchill, Never Give In
http://www.winstonchurchill.org/resources/speeches/1941-1945-war-leader/103-never-give-in

Winning is a Drug

What It Takes to be Number One
http://www.vincelombardi.com/number-one.html

THE WINNER EFFECT: THE SCIENCE OF SUCCESS AND HOW TO USE IT.
https://professorianrobertson.wordpress.com/books-by-ian/

'We Built It': The Neuroscience of Success
https://www.psychologytoday.com/blog/the-winner-effect/201209/we-built-it-the-neuroscience-success#_edn1

How power affects the brain
https://thepsychologist.bps.org.uk/volume-26/edition-3/how-power-affects-brain

Peter Thiel: Zero to One: Notes on Startups, or How to Build the Future
https://www.amazon.com/Zero-One-Notes-Startups-Future/dp/0804139296

Deliberate Practice

Anders Ericsson and Robert Pool, PEAK: SECRETS FROM THE NEW SCIENCE OF EXPERTISE
http://peakthebook.com/index.html

Malcolm Gladwell got us wrong: Our research was key to the 10,000-hour rule, but here's what got oversimplified
http://www.salon.com/2016/04/10/malcolm_gladwell_got_us_

wrong_our_research_was_key_to_the_10000_hour_rule_but_heres_what_got_oversimplified/

Malcolm Gladwell, Outliers http://gladwell.com/outliers/

Does Chess Need Intelligence?--A Study with Young Chess Players https://eric.ed.gov/?id=EJ772623

Ab Initio

Eli Goldratt, The Choice
https://www.amazon.com/Choice-Revised-Eliyahu-M-Goldratt/dp/0884271935/ref=pd_sbs_14_img_0?_encoding=UTF8&psc=1&refRID=2KDQKDQYDA56WP9MGGV2

Elon Musk's Surprising Strategy for Thinking About Everything
http://www.inc.com/quora/elon-musks-surprising-strategy-for-thinking-about-everything.html?cid=sf01002&sr_share=facebook

How Elon Musk Learns Faster and Better Than Everyone Else
http://observer.com/2016/09/how-elon-musk-learns-faster-and-better-than-everyone-else/

Elon Musk Uses This Ancient Critical-Thinking Strategy To Outsmart Everybody Else
http://www.businessinsider.com/elon-musk-first-principles-2015-1

Foundation 20 // Elon Musk
https://www.youtube.com/watch?v=L-s_3b5fRd8

Aristotle's First Principles
https://books.google.ru/books?id=8tYcp0vYd5EC&printsec=frontcover&source=gbs_ge_summary_r&cad=0#v=onepage&q&f=false

Learning Transfer

Bransford, J. D., Brown, A. L., & Cocking, R. R. (Eds.). (2000). Learning and transfer (Chapter 3). In How people learn: Brain, mind, experience, and school. Washington, DC: National Academy Press. [Online]. Available: https://www.nap.edu/catalog/9853/how-people-learn-brain-mind-experience-and-school-expanded-edition .

Learning and Transfer
https://people.ucsc.edu/~gwells/Files/Courses_Folder/ED%20261%20Papers/How%20People%20Learn%20Ch3.pdf

Lessons for Life: Learning and Transfer
https://www.learner.org/courses/learningclassroom/support/11_learning_transfer.pdf

Investors of Time

Steve Jobs' 2005 Stanford Commencement Address
https://www.youtube.com/watch?v=UF8uR6Z6KLc

Walter Isaacson, Steve Jobs, Simon & Schuster 2011
https://www.amazon.com/Steve-Jobs-Walter-Isaacson/dp/1451648537

Bridging Time and Length Scales in Materials Science and Bio-Physics
http://www.ipam.ucla.edu/programs/long-programs/bridging-time-and-length-scales-in-materials-science-and-bio-physics/

Fernan Braudel, On History
https://books.google.ru/books?id=AusOBEQZFXIC&printsec=frontcover&source=gbs_ge_summary_r&cad=0#v=onepage&q&f=false

Why time seems to fly – or trickle – by
https://theconversation.com/why-time-seems-to-fly-or-trickle-by-70515

Mihaly Csikszentmihalyi, Flow: The Psychology of Optimal Experience
https://www.amazon.com/Flow-Psychology-Experience-Perennial-Classics/dp/0061339202

Mihaly Csikszentmihalyi, Claremont Graduate University's Distinguished Professor of Psychology and Management.
https://www.cgu.edu/people/mihaly-csikszentmihalyi/

Erwin Schrodinger, What is Life
https://www.amazon.com/What-Life-Autobiographical-Sketches-Classics/dp/1107604664

Passion? Calling! Purpose! Passion!

Steve Jobs talks iPhone - All Things D5 (2007)
https://www.youtube.com/watch?v=fkPN_UoD3CM

8 smart pieces of advice from Elon Musk and 3 other powerful billionaires
http://www.businessinsider.com/pieces-of-advice-from-elon-musk-and-other-powerful-billionaires-2015-2

Amazon CEO, Jeff Bezos, sat down with Henry Blodget at Business Insider's Ignition 2014
https://www.youtube.com/watch?v=Xx92bUw7WX8

Entrepreneur Network partner Bryan Elliott sits down with WeWork co-founder, Miguel McKelvey
https://www.youtube.com/watch?v=vzWTzHhRkSU

Thiel - Following a calling is better than being passionate.
https://www.youtube.com/watch?v=kCtojhANxZk

Pursuit of Happiness, In the Zone

Flow in Sports by Susan Jackson, Mihaly Csikszentmihalyi
http://www.humankinetics.com/products/all-products/flow-in-sports

What do athletes mean by 'playing in the zone?'
http://www.sportingnews.com/other-sports/news/what-does-in-the-zone-mean-athletes-peak-performances/1kugz4tuad8j513rgnpophp65q

Athletes 'in the zone' report intense awareness, time transformation
http://www.sportingnews.com/other-sports/news/the-psychology-behind-athletes-being-in-the-zone-kobe-bryant-brett-favre/1h9atojwhoe75i0jbrol6qbqwn

"To strive, to seek, to find, and not to yield"

'To strive, to seek, to find, and not to yield': Tennyson, 'Ulysses', and the Olympics
https://blogs.surrey.ac.uk/english/2012/08/02/to-strive-to-seek-to-find-and-not-to-yield-tennyson-ulysses-and-the-olympics/

MiB: Danny Kahneman on Heuristics, Biases & Cognition
http://ritholtz.com/2016/08/mib-kahneman-heuristics-biases-cognition/

Amazing Amazon Story - Jeff Bezos Full Speech
https://www.youtube.com/watch?v=YlgkfOr_GLY&t=64s

"Screw It, Let's Do It"

Forbes/profile/Richard Branson
https://www.forbes.com/profile/richard-branson/

https://www.virgin.com/richard-branson/action-breeds-confidence

David Meets Goliath

Goliath https://en.wikipedia.org/wiki/Goliath

1 Samuel 17
https://www.biblegateway.com/passage/?search=1+Samuel+17

Chapter 28: David and Goliath
https://www.lds.org/manual/old-testament-stories/chapter-28-david-and-goliath?lang=eng

God Does not Play Dice, Billionaires Do

Forbes/Profile/Jeff Bezos
https://www.forbes.com/profile/jeff-bezos/

Amazing Amazon Story - Jeff Bezos Full Speech
https://www.youtubc.com/watch?v=YlgkfOr_GLY&t=64s

Entrepreneur Network partner Bryan Elliott sits down with WeWork co-founder, Miguel McKelvey
https://www.youtube.com/watch?v=vzWTzHhRkSU

Prigogine, Ilya and Isabelle Stengers. Order out of Chaos, University of Michigan: Bantam Books (1984)
https://deterritorialinvestigations.files.wordpress.com/2015/03/ilya_prigogine_isabelle_stengers_alvin_tofflerbookfi-org.pdf

Forbes/Profile/Miguel McKelvey
https://www.forbes.com/profile/miguel-mckelvey/

Bayesian Probabilities

Bayesian Statistics explained to Beginners in Simple English
https://www.analyticsvidhya.com/blog/2016/06/bayesian-statistics-beginners-simple-english/

The Quantum Origin of Time
http://www.bbc.com/earth/story/20160708-the-past-is-not-set-in-stone-so-we-may-be-able-to-change-it

Markov Process

Andrey Markov https://en.wikipedia.org/wiki/Andrey_Markov

Markov chain https://en.wikipedia.org/wiki/Markov_chain

The Quantum Origin of Time
http://www.bbc.com/earth/story/20160708-the-past-is-not-set-in-stone-so-we-may-be-able-to-change-it

50/50

Business Employment Dynamics/Establishment survival
https://www.bls.gov/bdm/entrepreneurship/entrepreneurship.htm

Do nine out of 10 new businesses fail, as Rand Paul claims?
https://www.washingtonpost.com/news/fact-checker/wp/2014/01/27/do-9-out-of-10-new-businesses-fail-as-rand-paul-claims/?utm_term=.41064552c79f

Debunking 'Black Swan' Events Of 2016
http://www.forbes.com/sites/nikolaikuznetsov/2017/01/15/debunking-black-swan-events-of-2016/2/#51dde8bf5e8d

Stopping Time

Stopping time https://en.wikipedia.org/wiki/Stopping_time

Monty Hall Problem

Monty Hall problem
https://en.wikipedia.org/wiki/Monty_Hall_problem

Understanding the Monty Hall Problem
https://betterexplained.com/articles/understanding-the-monty-hall-problem/

Where Nurture Meets Nature

Philosophie Zoologique (1809), Vol. 1, 235, trans. Hugh Elliot (1914), 113.

Epigenetics and the Human Brain: Where Nurture Meets Nature
https://www.ncbi.nlm.nih.gov/pmc/articles/PMC3574773/

Jean-Baptiste Lamarck (1744-1829)
http://www.ucmp.berkeley.edu/history/lamarck.html

X-Men

X-Men https://en.wikipedia.org/wiki/X-Men

X-Men http://marvel.com/characters/71/x-men

X-Men: Apocalypse/Quotes
http://www.imdb.com/title/tt3385516/quotes

In Video, Uber CEO Argues With Driver Over Falling Fares
https://www.bloomberg.com/news/articles/2017-02-28/in-video-uber-ceo-argues-with-driver-over-falling-fares

A profound apology
https://newsroom.uber.com/a-profound-apology/

Uber Driver Fawzi Kamel Explains Why He Argued With CEO Kalanick
http://www.nbcnews.com/news/us-news/uber-driver-fawzi-kamel-explains-why-he-argued-firm-s-n727496

Babes & Balls

Uber CEO Travis Kalanick played ping pong with Mark Zuckerberg at a party called 'Babes and Balls'
http://www.businessinsider.com/travis-kalanick-and-mark-zuckerberg-played-ping-pong-at-a-babes-and-balls-party-2017-3

Houston, Kalanick and Zuck walk into a headline
https://techcrunch.com/2017/03/10/houston-kalanick-and-zuck-walk-into-a-headline/

Susan Fowler, the techie taking on Uber
https://www.ft.com/content/469fbaec-fa76-11e6-9516-2d969e0d3b65

Uber says it's 'absolutely not' behind a smear campaign against ex-employee Susan Fowler Rigetti
https://techcrunch.com/2017/02/24/uber-says-its-absolutely-not-behind-a-smear-campaign-against-ex-employee-susan-fowler-rigetti/

Arianna Huffington: Sexual Harassment Isn't a 'Systemic Problem' at Uber
http://fortune.com/2017/03/21/arianna-huffington-sexual-harassment-uber/

The Mutation

Dopamine Turns Worker Ants Into Warrior Queens
https://news.ncsu.edu/2014/05/penick-gamergates-2014/

Epigenetic changes in the developing brain: Effects on behavior
http://www.pnas.org/content/112/22/6789.full

The Future of Neuroepigenetics in the Human Brain
https://www.ncbi.nlm.nih.gov/pmc/articles/PMC4863594/

Epigenetics in the Human Brain
http://www.nature.com/npp/journal/v38/n1/full/npp201278a.html

Can we observe epigenetic effects on human brain function?
https://www.ncbi.nlm.nih.gov/pmc/articles/PMC4486509/#R49

Tetrahedra

Definition of 'tetrahedron'
https://www.collinsdictionary.com/dictionary/english/tetrahedron

Tetrahedron https://en.wikipedia.org/wiki/Tetrahedron

Digital Alchemist' Seeks Rules of Emergence
https://www.quantamagazine.org/20170308-digital-alchemist-sharon-glotzer-interview-emergence/

Where now?

A message from Ilya Prigogine
http://firstmonday.org/ojs/index.php/fm/article/view/687/597

Snapchat's three-part business model with CEO Evan Spiegel (2015 Code Conference, Day 1)
https://www.youtube.com/watch?v=AqPHordzhdw

Snapchat https://en.wikipedia.org/wiki/Snapchat

Anternet

What Do Ants Know That We Don't?

https://www.wired.com/2013/07/what-ants-yes-know-that-we-dont-the-future-of-networking/

The Regulation of Ant Colony Foraging Activity without Spatial Information

http://journals.plos.org/ploscompbiol/article?id=10.1371/journal.pcbi.1002670

'Anternet' discovered: Behavior of harvester ants as they forage for food mirrors protocols that control Internet traffic

https://www.sciencedaily.com/releases/2012/08/120829094209.htm

Traffic control: What we can learn from ants

https://www.sciencedaily.com/releases/2015/04/150422084350.htm

Simple Complexity

Forbes/Profile/Jack Ma

https://www.forbes.com/profile/jack-ma/

What Do Ants Know That We Don't?

https://www.wired.com/2013/07/what-ants-yes-know-that-we-dont-the-future-of-networking/

Collective intelligence: Ants and brain's neurons

http://news.stanford.edu/pr/93/931115Arc3062.html

Jack Ma Davos Interview: Harvard rejected me 10 times!

https://www.youtube.com/watch?v=o5BKaDCda_0

Steve Jobs on Apple's resurgence
http://allaboutstevejobs.com/sayings/stevejobsinterviews/bw98.php

Brain-to-Brain coupling: A mechanism for creating and sharing a social world
https://www.ncbi.nlm.nih.gov/pmc/articles/PMC3269540/

Coupled Brains

Brain-to-Brain coupling: A mechanism for creating and sharing a social world
https://www.ncbi.nlm.nih.gov/pmc/articles/PMC3269540/

Good to Great. Article
http://www.jimcollins.com/article_topics/articles/good-to-great.html

To Alpha Centauri

Social class affects neural empathic responses
https://asumaclab.files.wordpress.com/2014/08/social-class-affects-neural-empathic-responses.pdf

How Wealth Reduces Compassion
https://www.scientificamerican.com/article/how-wealth-reduces-compassion/

Internet investor Yuri Milner joins with Berkeley in $100 million search for extraterrestrial intelligence
http://news.berkeley.edu/2015/07/20/breakthrough-search-for-extraterrestrial-intelligence/

INTERNET INVESTOR AND SCIENCE PHILANTHROPIST YURI MILNER & PHYSICIST STEPHEN HAWKING ANNOUNCE BREAKTHROUGH STARSHOT PROJECT TO DEVELOP 100 MILLION MILE PER HOUR MISSION TO THE

STARS WITHIN A GENERATION
https://breakthroughinitiatives.org/News/4

BREAKTHROUGH PRIZE MARKS 5TH ANNIVERSARY
CELEBRATING TOP ACHIEVEMENTS IN SCIENCE AND
AWARDS MORE THAN $25 MILLION IN PRIZES AT GALA
CEREMONY IN SILICON VALLEY
https://breakthroughprize.org/News/34

Tech Billionaires Award $25 Million in Breakthrough Prizes to
Top Scientists
http://fortune.com/2016/12/04/breakthrough-prize-science-win
ners-tech-billionaires/

The Giving Pledge is a commitment by the world's wealthiest
individuals and families to dedicate the majority of their wealth
to philanthropy. https://givingpledge.org

Warren Buffett says these billionaires' letters might be more
valuable than their money
http://www.businessinsider.com/warren-buffett-says-giving-ple
dge-letters-are-more-valuable-than-money-2016-9

JP's Peace, Love and Happiness Foundation
http://peacelovehappinessfoundation.org

Why Billionaire John Paul DeJoria's Rok Mobile Is Pairing Life
And Burial Insurance With A $49 Plan
http://www.forbes.com/sites/chloesorvino/2016/05/11/why-bill
ionaire-john-paul-dejorias-rok-mobile-is-pairing-life-and-burial-
insurance-with-a-49-plan/#1c8a66d236b5

Mark Zuckerberg and Priscilla Chan's $3 billion effort aims to rid
world of major diseases by end of century
https://www.washingtonpost.com/news/to-your-health/wp/201

6/09/21/mark-zuckerberg-and-priscilla-chans-3-billion-scientific-effort-aims-to-rid-world-of-major-diseases-by-end-of-century/?utm_term=.2bd49199cece

Sean Parker Launches an Unprecedented Cancer Research Effort
http://fortune.com/2016/04/13/parker-institute-launch-cancer-immunotherapy/

Facebook shares: what's behind Mark Zuckerberg's 'hacker philanthropy'?
https://www.theguardian.com/technology/2015/dec/02/facebook-shares-whats-behind-mark-zuckerbergs-hacker-philanthropy

Dopamine Turns Worker Ants Into Warrior Queens
https://news.ncsu.edu/2014/05/penick-gamergates-2014/

And beyond..

Elon Musk's revolt against futurist-led A.I. Apocalypse
http://www.trunews.com/article/elon-musks-revolt-against-futurist-led-a.i.-apocalypse#sthash.XErcYz6A.dpuf

Lazy Ants Make Colonies More Productive
https://www.seekcr.com/lazy-ants-make-colonies-more-productive-2199658973.html

Happiness of Understanding

Fireside chat with Google co-founders, Larry Page and Sergey Brin with Vinod Khosla
https://www.youtube.com/watch?v=Wdnp_7atZoM

www.ingramcontent.com/pod-product-compliance
Lightning Source LLC
Chambersburg PA
CBHW050450290526

45786CB00006B/2237

*9 7 8 1 5 4 5 3 4 4 1 7 0 *